D1473599

MODERN WORLD NATIONS

Panama

Charles F. Gritzner
and
Linnea C. Swanson

CHELSEA HOUSE
PUBLISHERS
An imprint of Infobase Publishing

Dedication

For Alan and Lee Swanson, who gave their daughter wings of curiosity to explore and a desire to better understand the fascinating world in which we live.

Frontispiece: Flag of Panama

Cover: Panama City, Panama

Panama

Copyright © 2008 by Infobase Publishing

Chelsea House
An imprint of Infobase Publishing
132 West 31st Street
New York NY 10001

Library of Congress Cataloging-in-Publication Data

Gritzner, Charles F.
  Panama / Charles F. Gritzner and Linnea C. Swanson.
    p. cm. — (Modern world nations)
  Includes bibliographical references and index.
  ISBN 978-0-7910-9673-4
  1. Panama—Juvenile literature. I. Swanson, Linnea C., 1985– II. Title. III. Series.

  F1563.2.G75 2008
  972.87—dc22   2007047569

Chelsea House books are available at special discounts when purchased in bulk quantities for businesses, associations, institutions, or sales promotions. Please call our Special Sales Department in New York at (212) 967-8800 or (800) 322-8755.

You can find Chelsea House on the World Wide Web at http://www.chelseahouse.com

Series design by Takeshi Takahashi
Cover design by Jooyoung An

Printed in the United States of America

Bang NMSG 10 9 8 7 6 5 4 3 2 1

Table of Contents

Panama

Welcome to Panama

Welcome to Panama: the world's most important cross-road! Panama is an anomaly. In terms of both size and population, the country should be little more than an unimportant "blip" on the global radar screen. In area, its 30,193 square-mile (78,200 square-kilometer) area makes it smaller than South Carolina, or about the same size as Canada's New Brunswick Province. With just over three million people, Panama's population is slightly smaller than that of metropolitan Atlanta, Georgia, or Toronto, Ontario. Yet this tiny country is one of the world's most important places. The Panama Canal has made the country a giant among nations in terms of its strategic importance.

Panama occupies a narrow, S-shaped ribbon of land that joins North and South America. It lies between Costa Rica, its Central American neighbor to the northwest and Colombia, South America's northwesternmost country. Historically, this position has made Panama an important crossroads, or corridor, for migrating flora, fauna, and humans for thousands of years. The country also occupies a thin strip of land—the Isthmus of Panama— that forms a land barrier between the Caribbean Sea (Atlantic Ocean) and the Pacific Ocean. At its narrowest point, the isthmus separates the two oceans by a distance of only about 38 miles (60 kilometers); at its widest point, it is about 110 miles (177 kilometers) across.

Placed within a larger spatial context, Panama falls within several regions. Its latitudinal position, roughly 8 to 10 degrees north latitude, places the country squarely in the tropics of the Northern Hemisphere. Historically, it belongs to the "New World," those lands discovered by Europeans who, beginning in the fifteenth century, sailed from the "Old World" (the known Afro-Eurasian land mass). Culturally, it falls within Latin America—a region settled largely by Spaniards (and Portuguese in Brazil), people from Europe's Iberian Peninsula. Panama also lies within Central America, a geographic region composed of small countries (sometimes called the Banana Republics) sandwiched between Mexico and South America. Additionally, the country is a part of Middle America, a region composed of Mexico, Central America, and the islands of the Caribbean. Lastly, those islands and mainland countries facing the Caribbean Sea constitute a region many geographers call Caribbean America.

Panama lacks physical extremes. Its land features are neither spectacular nor threatening. Unlike most countries lying on the Pacific "Ring of Fire," Panama rarely experiences earthquakes or volcanic eruptions. The tropical climate offers few hardships and the country lies well to the south of paths taken by devastating hurricanes. The most noteworthy physical aspect of Panama is its narrow width, an isthmus that separates the Atlantic and Pacific oceans by only a short distance.

Historically, Panama became the earliest site of successful Spanish settlement on the mainland of the Americas. Perhaps

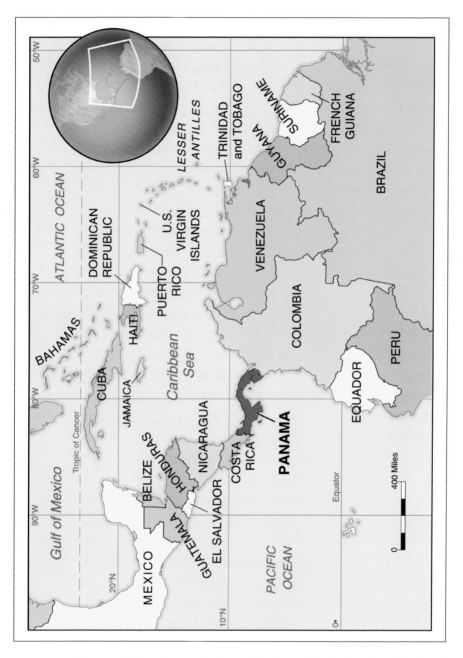

Panama bridges the gap between North and South America. Bordered on the north by the Caribbean Sea, on the east by Colombia, on the south by the Pacific Ocean, and on the west by Costa Rica, it is slightly smaller than South Carolina.

the country's most important historical event occurred in 1513. In that year, Vasco Nuñez de Balboa crossed the isthmus and discovered (from the Americas) the Pacific Ocean. As Spanish power and influence grew in the New World, Panama's importance grew. The isthmus became an important crossroad between Spain, the Caribbean Basin, and Spanish colonies lying on the Pacific shore of the Americas. This role and its importance would vastly expand through time.

The country's history, however, has been anything but placid. Because of its strategic location and function, Panama has often been a pawn controlled by outside forces.

Panamanian culture—its people and their way of life—is a vibrant mix of Amerindian, Spanish, African, and other traits. The dominant Spanish language and Roman Catholic faith practiced by the country's people reflect early Spanish influences. Today, many of Panama's people are undergoing a slow and often difficult cultural transition. They are leaving the countryside and a mainly self-sufficient, traditional way of life (folk culture) and moving to the city, which imposes an entirely new set of cultural demands. Most rural Panamanians are flocking to the country's capital, Panama City, which is a modern, cosmopolitan center with a population that now exceeds one million.

In Panama, government and economy are closely intertwined. A substantial portion of the country's income is generated by the Panama Canal. And directly or indirectly, many people owe their jobs to the canal and business that it brings to the country. Today, Panama still has a small number of *Amerindians*—American Indians—who practice a very traditional economy based upon hunting, fishing, gathering, and rudimentary farming. At the other extreme, the contemporary postindustrial service sector of the country's economy is booming.

Life has seldom, if ever, been better for Panamanians. For the first time in decades (and some would say ever), some

Panama City, the capital and largest city in the Republic of Panama, is located at the Pacific entrance of the Panama Canal. The city has topped several key regional rankings within the past few years, including being named the most globalized city and the fastest-growing city in Latin America.

semblance of stability has settled upon the country's oftentimes turbulent political system and government. The economy is growing at a robust 8 to 9 percent each year (as of 2007). In mainland Latin America, only Venezuela and Argentina are experiencing a comparable rate of economic growth. With work now underway on enlarging the canal, the economy should continue to grow at a fast pace for some time. Most Panamanians now look to the future with considerable optimism.

Imagine yourself as being an engineer or a builder. You are given an assignment: build a canal that links the Atlantic and Pacific oceans. In preparing for the task, you learn that one of the world's leading countries already failed dismally at the task. During the project, an estimated 22,500 people have lost their lives to deadly tropical diseases.

You must construct a canal that passes through 48 miles (77 kilometers) of solid rock and unstable earth subject to landslides. At the continental divide, you will be confronted by a land barrier nearly 400 feet (120 meters) above sea level. Even by excavating a huge trench, you still must be able to "lift" huge ships 85 feet (26 meters) above sea level. To achieve this, you must build a series of locks that can fill and be emptied to raise and lower vessels.

Where will you find the water to fill the locks? A dam must be built and a reservoir created to provide the water. Meanwhile, laborers must be found and the political situation must be stabilized. Diseases must be eradicated. And the infrastructure must be put in place to begin what would be the most difficult construction project in history. When completed (in 1914), the Panama Canal would reduce the sailing distance between the two oceans by about 8,000 miles (12,875 kilometers). In this book, the authors have divided the canal into several segments: the physical aspects are discussed in Chapter 2; the historical and political developments, appearing in Chapter 3; and the economic significance of the canal is discussed in Chapter 5.

Are you ready to begin your journey through Panama? If so, your trip will begin with a tour of the country's physical conditions and landscapes. ¡Bienvenido a Panama! (Welcome to Panama!)

CHAPTER

2

Physical Landscapes

You might wonder what Panama's physical geography, Hudson Bay, the Arctic Ocean, Magellan, and the southern tip of South America have in common. Christopher Columbus thought he had reached the East Indies, hence, the name "Indians" for the American aborigines. Soon, however, explorers began to realize that rather than the riches of the Orient, Columbus had stumbled upon a huge barrier lying between Europe and the Indies.

THE ISTHMUS OF PANAMA

For centuries, the search for a route through or around the Americas occupied the attention of numerous European countries and explorers. In his epic 1519–1522 voyage, Ferdinand Magellan sailed through the strait that bears his name near the southern tip of South America. But the route involved vast distance and some of the world's most treacherous seas. These factors made the passage to and through the Strait of Magellan both extremely dangerous and very costly in terms of time and expense. During the sixteenth and seventeenth centuries, Henry Hudson was but one of many hardy explorers who searched for the elusive Northwest Passage. This much sought-after route, around the northern margin of North America, also ended in frustration. The frozen waters of the Arctic Ocean proved to be an insurmountable obstacle to such a passage.

From very early times in their New World experience, Spaniards took advantage of Panama's *isthmian* shape. At its narrowest points, the isthmus (a narrow parcel of land between two seas) is only about 30 to 50 miles (50 to 80 kilometers) wide. They used the isthmus as the shortest and easiest route between the Caribbean and their Pacific-facing colonies. A narrow ribbon of land may seem like an insignificant aspect of a country's physical geography. Yet, through time, this thin strip of land resulted in Panama becoming one of Earth's most strategic locations. For some 350 years, crossings were by foot or animal-pulled wagons. Eventually, these slow and rather primitive means gave way to more modern transportation. A railroad spanned the isthmus in 1855; the Panama Canal opened in 1914. Later, a trans-isthmian pipeline was completed in 1982; currently the canal is being enlarged, which is scheduled for completion in 2014 or 2015.

LAND FEATURES

In some ways, Panama is deceiving. In Panama City, for example, the sun rises over the Pacific. And from atop Cerro Jefe (also called Balboa Hill), a low mountain near Panama City, both the Atlantic and Pacific oceans can be seen from the same location. And, yes, from this point the sun *rises* over the Pacific and *sets* over the Atlantic—the only place in the world where this occurs! If you passed through the Panama Canal from the Caribbean to the Pacific Ocean, in what direction do you think you would travel? Would you ever guess north*west* to south*east*? Are you confused? Perhaps looking at a map of Panama can help explain the foregoing anomalies.

Panama's narrow, rather scrawny, semi-S-shaped form extends in a roughly east-west direction, rather than north-south. Can you see, for example, how someone on the east coast of the Peninsula de Azuero (that juts into the Pacific) would watch the sun rise over the Pacific? Or imagine that you are along the Caribbean coast west of Colón. Do you see how the sun would set over the Golfo de los Mosquitoes, in the Atlantic Ocean?

Panama's land features are dominated by low mountains. Most of the country is formed by uplands, leaving very few areas of lowland plains. Only about 7 percent of Panama is relatively flat land that is well suited to mechanized agriculture. The largest expanses of plains are in the southwest near David and along the western side of the Gulf of Panama. Elsewhere, hills and mountains dominate the physical landscape. Several mountain ranges extend eastward from Costa Rica to the canal. Although they are recognized by local names, collectively, they are called the Cordillera Central by Panamanian geographers. The country's highest elevation is located in the Cordillera de Talamanca, one of the several ranges that form the Cordillera Central. Here, north of the city of David, Volcán Barú (formerly named Volcán de Chiriquí), rises to an elevation of 11,401 feet (3,475 meters). Although a volcano, Barú has not been active for thousands of years.

A slight gap, with elevations lower than 300 feet (90 meters), exists at the point where the canal crosses the isthmus. East of the canal, toward Colombia, elevations rise once again. Along the Caribbean coast, the Cordillera San Blas attains an elevation of about 3,000 feet (900 meters). (Both cordillera and serranía are Spanish terms for mountain ranges.) Without a noticeable break, the range closely hugs the Caribbean coast and contin-ues into Colombia as the Serranía del Darién. To the south, the

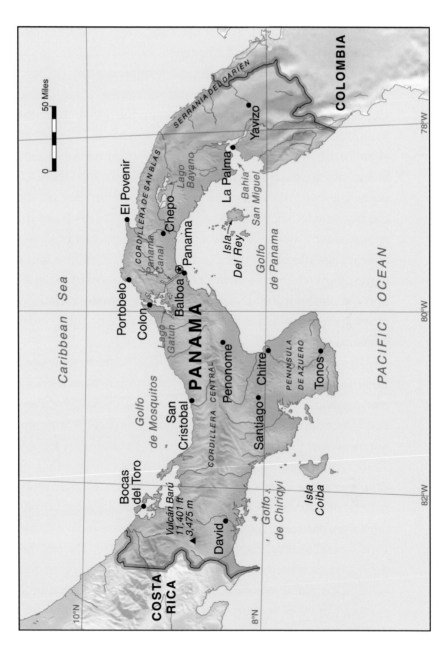

Panama has a diverse landscape. There is a chain of mountains in the west, hills in the interior, and coastal regions along a considerable portion of the country. Forests cover nearly 60 percent of the land area and the dormant Volcán Barú rises 11,398 feet (3,475 meters) above sea level.

low Serranía del Sapo borders the Pacific and continues into Colombia as the Serranía del Baudó.

Panama has two other physical features worthy of note. One is the rather large, southward extending "bump" that reaches into the Pacific to the west of the canal. It is the Península Azuero, a somewhat rugged upland that reaches an elevation of about 3,000 feet (900 meters). Another interesting feature of Panama is the hundreds of islands that dot its coastal zone. The two major archipelagos (island chains) are on the Caribbean side. The more than 350 San Blas islands extend for approximately 100 miles (160 kilometers) from east of Colón to near the Colombia border. In the west, near the Costa Rican border, the Archipiélago de Bocas del Toro (Mouths of the Bull) dots the coast north of David. These islands remain a relatively unspoiled tropical paradise that is becoming a popular center of environmentally friendly ecotourism.

The Pacific side of Panama is dotted with an estimated 1,000 islands. Archipiélago de las Perlas (Pearl Islands) is an island group in the Gulf of Panama, just off the coast of Panama City. Some of the world's finest pearls have come from the waters adjacent to the islands.

Isla de Coiba, west of Península Azuero in the Gulf of Chiriquí, is the largest island in all of Central America. From 1919 to 2004, it was the site of a notorious penal colony. Conditions were particularly brutal during the dictatorships of Omar Torrijos and Manuel Noriega from 1969 to 1989. During this period, an estimated 300 political prisoners were tortured and killed in the island prison. In 1992 the island became a national park and in 2005 the park was named a World Heritage Site. Waters surrounding the island offer outstanding deep-sea diving, snorkeling, and deep-sea fishing.

WEATHER AND CLIMATE

Panama's latitudinal position between 7 degrees and 10 degrees north latitude places the country squarely within the tropics.

Here, a prison guard watches over a beachside camp on Coiba Island (Isla de Coiba). During the dictatorships of Omar Torrijos and Manuel Noriega, this island was a prison with a reputation for brutal conditions, extreme tortures, executions, and political murder. Shut down in 2004, it is now a national park and the home of rare flora and fauna.

Overall, the climate is oppressively hot and humid throughout the year and in most locations. Heat and moisture combine to create an extremely monotonous climate. Weather conditions vary little throughout the year. Nonetheless, some differences do occur throughout the country. Conditions are much wetter and more humid along the northern Caribbean coast than in the south. Here, a wet tropical climate prevails. To the south, along the Pacific, temperatures continue to be quite high throughout the year. But the region receives somewhat less moisture and has a short dry season. This zone is classified as having a wet-and-dry tropical climate. Uplands, with their cooler temperatures, offer still a third set of conditions: a tropical highlands climate.

TEMPERATURE

Surprisingly, the tropical latitudes do not have the world's highest extreme temperatures. This can be explained by two factors. First, near the equator the sun rises around (solar) 6:00 A.M. and sets at about (solar) 6:00 P.M. Therefore, the sun is only above the horizon for about 12 hours. The farther poleward from the equator one goes the longer the period of sunlight. Because the sun is above the horizon for a much longer time during the summer months in the midlatitudes, considerably higher temperatures occur. (The world's record high temperature is 136.4°F [58°C], recorded in the Sahara Desert.) The tropical climates do, however, experience the highest annual average temperatures. In middle and poleward latitudes, averages are lower because of winter low temperatures.

The second reason is that with the constantly moist atmosphere, clouds form during the hottest period of the day. They serve as a shield against the sunlight resulting in less solar energy hitting Earth's surface and being converted to heat. This results in somewhat cooler temperatures than would occur with a clear sky. Finally, temperatures decrease with increased elevation at a rate of about 3.5°F per 1,000 feet (6.5°C/1,000 meters).

The average annual temperature in both Panama City and Colón is about 81°F (26°C). Daily highs range from an average 85° to 87°F (29° to 30°C) and daily lows from 73° to 75°F (23°C). In Panama City, the all-time record high temperature is 100°F (38°C) and the low is 63°F (17.5°C), a range of only 37 degrees (20.5°C). Temperatures above 90°F (32°C) are very rare, as are those below 70°F (21°C). Upland temperatures are cooler and more pleasant. An upland valley located at about 3,000 feet (300 meters), for example, would experience a temperature about 10 degrees (5°C) cooler than a location at sea level. Higher elevations in the Cordillera Central experience occasional frost.

PRECIPITATION

The greatest differences in Panama's patterns of weather and climate are related to moisture. In fact, Panamanians identify seasons not by temperature, but by rainfall. From May to January, rain falls almost daily and humidity is high, 80 percent or more. A short dry season extends from February through April. These dates may vary by a month or two from year to year and place to place within the country. The northern Caribbean half of the country is much wetter—nearly twice as moist—than the southern half that faces the Pacific. Colón, for example, averages about 130 inches (330 centimeters) of rainfall a year. Less than 50 miles (80 kilometers) to the southeast, Panama City receives an average of 70 inches (178 centimeters) of precipitation annually.

The slight seasonal differences can be explained by shifts in pressure and wind systems that affect the region's weather and climate. During the short drier season, the sun is lower in the sky, resulting in less warming and convectional activity. Also, the northeast trade winds weaken slightly. The reason the southern half of Panama is somewhat drier than the northern side can easily be explained by the country's mountainous backbone. Warm, moist, northeast trade winds blowing onshore off the Caribbean are forced aloft over the coastal mountains. This is what geographers refer to as the *orographic* effect. As the wind forces the air aloft, it cools, condenses (changes from vapor to liquid), and drops much of its moisture on the windward (northern and northeastern) side of mountain slopes. As the winds descend toward the southern and southwestern half of the country, they begin to warm. In what is called the *rain shadow* effect, warming air increases its moisture-holding capability; hence, it is much less apt to condense and precipitate.

Nearly all rainfall, at all locations, and during all seasons is in the form of convectional thundershowers, some of which can be severe. Occasionally, such showers contribute to local

Because of its unique location between two continents, Panama is home to several animal species not found anywhere else. It has one of the most diverse populations of birds in the world, making it a great place for bird watching. Pictured here is the Keel-billed Toucan (also known as the Rainbow-billed Toucan), which is mainly found in the canopies of tropical, subtropical, and lowland rain forests.

flooding conditions. Fortunately, Panama lies to the south of the Atlantic hurricane path. These devastating storms travel well to the north, although they do frequently strike other Central American countries.

ECOSYSTEMS

Panama's moist tropical climate supports some of the world's most lush vegetation and an abundance of wildlife unmatched elsewhere in North America. The country is home to more than three times as many plant and animal species than are found in the United States, Canada, and Europe combined. About 40 percent of the country has a dense cover of tropical rain forest.

Rain forests thrive in the northwest, along much of the north coast and throughout most of the eastern half of Panama. The rain forest, or *selva*, is much different than the midlatitude forests with which most readers are familiar. The following features and conditions are characteristic of this unique ecosystem:

- **Many species grow within a small area.** As many as 400 tree species can live within a single square mile area. This diversity makes it difficult if not impossible to locate and harvest a particular economically valuable species, such as mahogany.

- **Most tree species are broadleaf evergreens.** In the tropics, there are few seasonal changes to trigger plant dormancy. As a result, the trees (most of which are broadleaf, rather than needle leaf) lose their leaves continuously throughout the year. A single tree may experience all seasonal growth stages at once.

- **Forests are three-tiered with a dense overhead canopy.** The rain forest is characterized by three tiers or levels of vegetation. Emergents, the tallest trees in the forest, may reach heights of 200 feet (60 meters). A second level reaches heights of 80 to 120 feet (25 to 35 meters) when mature. Finally, the lowest trees reach a height of only 40 to 60 feet (10 to 20 meters) when full grown. The dense overhead canopy blocks sunlight, causing light at ground level to be a dull eerie green. Because there is very little sunlight, the forest floor has very little plant life.

- **Some species have unique characteristics.** Buttresses that flare outward at the base of the trunk are common among many tropical tree species. Some buttresses are quite small, but others may reach 25 feet (7.5 meters) up the trunk and flare

out 10 to 20 feet (3 to 6 meters) from the base.
Many trees have long, straight trunks with few if
any lower branches. Toward their top, the crown
flares outward in a fashion that closely resembles an
umbrella. Along the coasts, mangroves have dozens
of stilt-like roots that rise above the water to support each tree. The complex mangrove root system
causes silt in the water to settle out. In this way,
they play a vital role in protecting coastal zones.

- **Each tree is host to a vast array of other plants.**
  Each rain forest tree plays host to many thousands
  of living organisms. Most trees are festooned with
  hundreds of vines (*lianas*), creepers, and dangling
  root systems hanging down from plants high above.
  Some of the plants are parasites that both cling to
  and gain their nourishment from their host. Others
  are *epiphytic.* They attach themselves to the host for
  support, but do not get their nourishment from the
  tree. Roots of epiphytes are a common sight as they
  dangle in midair to draw moisture and nourishment from the atmosphere.

- **Plant life changes with increased elevation.** Many
  tropical plants have a very limited habitat (the
  environment in which an organism can live).
  With increased elevation, temperatures become
  cooler, hence, habitats change. Tropical rain forest seldom occurs above 3,500 feet (1,070 meters).
  In upland regions, there is often a narrow vertical
  zone that experiences almost constant fog. Under
  these conditions, a cloud forest, also called fairy
  or elfin forest, can develop. Because of the nearly
  constant 100 percent humidity, ferns, mosses, and
  other moisture-loving plants thrive. The result is
  plant life that takes on the appearance of a green
  fairyland.

There is a widely held myth that a jungle and a tropical rain forest are one and the same, but they are not. Edgar Rice Burroughs's *Tarzan* books seem to have been the origin of this misconception. Burroughs incorrectly referred to the rain forest as a jungle. Actually, the rain forest's thick overhead canopy blocks sunlight, which results in very little vegetation at ground level. Surprisingly, perhaps, the floor of the tropical rain forest is quite clear and open. Jungle is correctly used in reference to a very dense mass of almost impenetrable plant life. It is found only where sunlight reaches the forest floor, as along the edge of agricultural fields, rivers, roads, or villages.

Not all vegetation is rain forest. Particularly in the western half of the drier Pacific-facing portion of Panama, savanna grasslands and scrub woodlands dominate the natural vegetation. Savannas are tall grasses with scattered *pyrophytic* (fire-resistant) trees. The few trees that dot the savanna landscape provide a clue to the origin of this ecosystem: human-created fires. During the wet season, the vegetation grows profusely, but during the short dry season it dries out. In order to clear the land of coarse, parched, dead vegetation, native peoples, and later Spaniards, used fire. Repeated fires killed most trees and created an open environment that favored the growth of grasses. These lands are widely used for livestock grazing.

Animal life abounds in Panama. In fact, the country boasts of having more bird species (934) than all of the United States and Canada combined! Both saltwater and freshwater species of fish and other marine life are plentiful. Land fauna include several species of monkeys, slow-moving sloths, several kinds of cats, and rodents such as the agouti. Among the hundreds of insects are varieties that transmit various tropical diseases, including the Anopheles mosquito that is the vector for malaria. Alligators, various snakes (including both venomous and constrictors), and bats (which may transmit rabies) are among the less desirable types of fauna.

Tropical soils tend to be rather infertile. Nutrients they initially possessed or acquired through time get leached away by excessive precipitation. Exceptions occur in places where streams deposit silt, as in river valleys or along the coasts. In the southwest, lower amounts of precipitation contribute to more fertile soils that support the growing of crops. Only about 7 percent of Panama's territory is suitable for farming.

ENVIRONMENTAL PROBLEMS AND ISSUES

Panama, fortunately, does not have many environmental hazards. The country does not experience the repeated volcanic and earthquake events that frequently devastate so many Andean and Middle American countries. Hurricanes, which ravage much of the Caribbean Basin and Gulf Coast, pass well to the north of Panama. Occasional severe storms can cause local flood and wind damage. During the drier season, forest fires can occur. Usually, however, they are in areas of low population density and economic development, so their toll on property is minimal.

Environmental problems, however, do plague Panama. Deforestation is widespread. The country's tree cover has been reduced by about 50 percent during the past half century and woodlands continue to disappear at an alarming rate. Much of the deforestation results from land clearing for cattle ranching or traditional shifting subsistence cultivation. There is some commercial logging and, of course, clearing of land for urban and other types of development. Deforestation, particularly on mountain slopes, greatly increases soil erosion. In central Panama, erosion results in the silting (filling with sand) of streams which, in turn, flow into and threaten the Panama Canal. And as forests disappear, so, too, does valuable wildlife habitat. Runoff from agricultural fields pollutes streams and threatens coastal marine resources.

Panamanians are aware of their environmental treasures and are taking positive steps to protect their natural endowment. During recent decades, the country has established 15 national parks, reserves, or refuges. In fact, nearly 30 percent of the country's area is now protected, a figure equaled or surpassed by very few other Latin American countries.

PHYSICAL GEOGRAPHY OF THE PANAMA CANAL

Nearly two centuries ago, German geographer Alexander von Humboldt suggested a canal be built across Central America. Spain authorized the building of a canal and set the plans in motion; however, the idea was short-lived. Eventually, the need for an easy Atlantic–Pacific crossing became more apparent. Throughout the project, physical geography played a very important, demanding, and often devastating role. Difficult terrain, weather and climate, and insects and disease were also important factors, as was the fresh and salt water and tidal ranges in the oceans.

Selecting the location for an isthmian canal was not an easy task. Several sites were considered. Far north in Mexico, it was proposed that the Isthmus of Tehuantepec could be an ideal route. Another proposed route was in Nicaragua. It followed the San Juan River into Lake Nicaragua, on to Lake Managua, and then went by a short canal to the Pacific. A location in Panama east of the present canal was also considered. Finally, a route in Colombia was suggested that would follow the Atrato River and closely parallel the existing border between the two countries. In 1878, the existing site of the Panama Canal was selected by the French when Ferdinand de Lesseps began construction of a sea-level canal. The project lasted 11 years, but collapsed in 1889. More than 22,000 workers had died from oppressive heat and humidity and deadly diseases transmitted by tropical insects.

The French had attempted to build a sea-level canal, one that did not require locks to lift and lower ships crossing the land barrier by canal. From the very outset, this idea drew criticism. Some worried about the vastly different tidal ranges in the Caribbean and Pacific. Sea level is 7 to 16 inches (18 to 40 centimeters) lower on the Pacific side than on the Atlantic. What would prevent a rush of water between the two oceans when water was about 20 feet (6 meters) higher at one end of the canal than at the other during extreme tidal conditions? Another concern was the free exchange of marine flora and fauna between the two ocean basins. How would a sea-level canal change the ecology of the respective seas?

The United States decided to construct a 48-mile (77 kilometers) long canal that employed locks. This method allows vessels to "climb" to a height of 85 feet (26 meters), which is the highest level of the canal, and then descend gradually to sea level. Construction required massive excavation of earth material, including deep cuts through rock. The continental divide, for example, rose 360 feet (110 meters) above sea level. Ultimately, the Gaillard Cut (the largest of the project) reduced that elevation to 40 feet (12 meters) above sea level.

Water, of course, does not flow uphill. How would ships cross high and dry elevations? Once the canal and locks were dug, where would water come from to keep both full? Fortunately, the Río Chagres drained much of the area through which the canal would be built. Gatún Dam was constructed on its lower course to create a large reservoir, Lake Gatún. The lake provides the necessary water for the canal and its locks as the route rises to cross the backbone of the isthmus. It also serves as a freshwater "filter" that prevents saltwater organisms from passing between oceans.

The canal was constructed with a two-way set of paired locks that allow vessels to pass one another while traveling in opposite directions. Overall, the canal employs three sets of locks. On the Atlantic side, the Gatún set has three flights (locks) that lift vessels traveling between the Caribbean and Lake Gatún. On the south side, between the lake and the Pacific, there are two sets of locks, the Miraflores and the Pedro Miguel. The Miraflores locks with two steps and the Pedro Miguel locks with a single step, allowing ships to rise or descend as they pass between Lake Gatún and the Pacific. Each lock chamber is 110 feet (about 34 meters) wide and 1,050 feet (320 meters) long. Nearly 27 million gallons (more than 101,000 cubic meters) of water must enter the lock to raise vessels. The same amount must be drained from the lock to lower a ship. Since the 1960s,

Pictured is a container ship passing through the Miraflores locks in the Panama Canal. Ships passing through pay a toll based on weight, which total tens of thousands of dollars. Despite the cost, the savings in fuel and time make using the canal worth it.

many ships have been too large to pass through the existing canal. In the summer of 2007, work began to expand the route. Once again, the forces of human will and technology will be pitted against obstacles imposed by the natural environment.

CHAPTER

3

Panama
Through Time

In this chapter, you will travel through the corridors of time as you learn about Panama's historical geography. We must, after all, look to the past if we are to understand present-day conditions. And for those of you with a sharp eye for history, you may be in for some surprises! "History," as found in history books and history classes, focuses primarily on individuals, dates, and events with most, if not all, information coming from written documents. Geographers studying history, on the other hand, take a much broader view of the past. We look for any and all important events and changes that have had an impact on a country's geographic conditions and patterns. Our information comes from many sources, not just written records. Are you ready to begin your trip through time?

AN ISTHMIAN CORRIDOR FORMS

The historical geography of what is now Panama began about 3 million years ago. It was in the distant geologic past that the Isthmus of Panama was formed, creating a land link joining the North and South American continents. The formation of this "land bridge" had two major effects. First, it served as a natural dam that deterred the movement of marine life between the Atlantic and Pacific basins. Second, it made possible a two-way flow of both plant and animal life between the two huge land masses. Ancestors of the horse and camel, for example, moved northward into North America and eventually into Asia. The movement of flora and fauna between the continents is an exchange that continues today, although to a lesser degree. Through time, the narrow Isthmus of Panama (also called the Isthmus of Darién) played a major role in the country's development.

THE FIRST PANAMANIANS

Today, archaeologists are not certain when the first humans arrived in Panama. For that matter, scientists are not sure who they were, where they came from, by what route they arrived, or how they traveled. There are many more questions than answers when one searches for clues that would help us better understand who the earliest Americans, hence Panamanians, were. About all that is known for certain is that they came from someplace else. There is absolutely no scientific evidence to support a theory suggesting that humankind had its origin here in the Americas.

A half century ago, most social scientists believed that they knew who the earliest people were, where they came from, and the route they traveled. Hunters from Asia, they believed, crossed Beringia, also known as the Bering Land Bridge (land between what is now Russia and Alaska exposed when sea level dropped during the Ice Age), in pursuit of big game animals.

Upon reaching North America, the hunters turned southward passing through an ice-free corridor between two massive ice masses. According to this scenario, they finally reached the southwestern United States about 12,000 to 13,000 years ago. Gradually, these early humans continued moving eastward and southward. Eventually, during much more recent times, they filled in the remainder of the North and South American continents. This route, of course, would have taken these early migrants through Panama on their way to South America.

Today, some scientists doubt this theory. They believe that a route across Beringia through an ice-free corridor would have been far too cold and inhospitable for early humans. Now evidence suggests that the Americas were occupied by humans long before any gap appeared between the North American glaciers. This evidence that casts doubt upon the traditional hypothesis comes from various locations throughout Latin America. If early humans entered the Americas from the north, the oldest archaeological evidence should be found in North America. In fact, many sites have been dated to perhaps 13,000 to 20,000 years ago. Based upon recent archaeological discoveries, however, many of the oldest sites—found by some scientists to be 30,000 or more years old—are in *South* America!

Support is growing for the theory of a migration by early people that followed a coastal route for at least a part of their journey. During the Ice Age, sea level was about 400 feet (122 meters) lower than it is today. Relatively flat land on the narrow continental shelves—land that is now underwater—would have been high and dry. The exposed shelves would have created a fine natural route for early wanderers.

Although the full story of the earliest Americans may never be fully told. Regardless of the route taken, and assuming migrants came from the north, they would have touched upon the isthmus. It may have been an inland route, although travel would have been extremely difficult. Even today, the Darién

Gap—an area in eastern Panama adjacent to Colombia—is all but impassable. They may have followed the coast, walking on the rather wide continental shelf that would have been exposed above sea level. During some of their passage, they might have rafted, closely following the shoreline. If the archaeological dates from South America are correct, these early travelers just may have passed through the area some 30,000 years ago. Some of them may have stayed behind in what is now Panama.

INDIGENOUS CULTURES

When the Spaniards arrived in what is now Panama at the dawn of the sixteenth century, they found more than 60 different tribal groups scattered throughout the region. Major groups included the Chibcha, the San Blas, the Guaymí, and the Kuna. In this context, it is important to note that considerable confusion exists when one attempts to identify native peoples. Much of the problem comes from distinctions in language versus tribal affiliation (although they often are one and the same). Regardless, some of the people clearly had cultural ties with Mesoamerican (Mexico and Guatemala) groups to the north. Their language and way of life were similar to those of the Mayans, although by then the Mayan "high civilization" had long vanished. People of Mayan language and culture were widespread throughout southern Mexico and northern Central America. Other groups had obvious cultural ties with the Amerindians of Colombia, particularly those who spoke the Chibchan tongue. Still others had ties with Amerindians inhabiting the Caribbean.

Most of Panama's aboriginal people remained physically and culturally isolated from Europeans, some well into the twentieth century. Although some differences existed between and among groups (for example, hunting versus fishing as a source of protein), there also were many similarities. For

The greatest number of Kuna, one of the indigenous peoples of Panama, live on small islands in Kuna Yala, an Indian reserve in the Caribbean Sea. Today, there are about 50,000 Kuna in Panama and Colombia.

example, Amerindians lived in villages and had some arrangement of tribal leadership and governance. Unlike groups to the north in Mexico (such as the Aztecs) and to the south in Colombia (the Chibcha, for example) Panama's tribes practiced a very traditional, meager subsistence economy. They lived in small scattered villages, rather than large cities. Material possessions were few and most were quite crude. Some people were fishermen, others were skilled hunters. Among the latter, the blowgun with poison-tipped darts and bow and arrow were very effective weapons.

Farming, which may have been practiced for several thousands of years in the region, was a form of slash-and-burn shifting cultivation. This type of agriculture is widespread throughout the world's humid tropics even today. The dense woodland is cut over (or slashed with a machete, a long-bladed knife) and the debris is left to dry. Once dry, it is burned, leaving a field of stumps, branches, and other woody material scattered about. The ash adds nutrients to the soil's very low natural fertility. Crops are planted, but little attention is given to tending them, so most fields resemble weed patches. Bananas, manioc (a tuber), and beans are among the major crops grown and what is raised is strictly for subsistence, or the tiller's own family's consumption. After a period of several years, the heavily leached soils lose their fertility. The plot is shifted to a new location.

Throughout much of Latin America, the arrival of Europeans brought tremendous changes, including the loss of civilizations and massive loss of life. In Panama, many native peoples were scarcely affected. They continued to live very traditional lives far removed from Spanish influence.

EUROPEANS ARRIVE

In the early 1500s, a wave of explorers visited the area now known as Panama in search of wealth and treasures, such as gold. In 1501, Spaniard Rodrigo de Bastidas became the first known European to reach the isthmus. For this achievement, he is credited with the discovery of Panama. Bastidas was sailing along the northern coast of South America in search of gold when he reached the shores of Panama. His landfall was just to the east of today's Panama Canal. After exploring the coastal areas, Bastidas and his crew headed back to the West Indies. A year later, in 1502, Christopher Columbus sailed along the isthmus during his fourth voyage to the New World. He claimed the territory for Spain and explored several areas of the coast, naming one Puerto Bello (Portobelo), meaning "beautiful port." By the end of the sixteenth century, this site became a key Spanish port because it was not as vulnerable to attack as others had been. Columbus and his crew stayed in the area for less than a year, however, because they found the natives to be quite hostile.

In 1510, eight years after Columbus's visit to the isthmus, Martin Fernández de Encisco sailed to the region. Vasco Nuñez de Balboa had told him of the friendly natives, fertile land, and adequate water supplies on the Gulf of Darién. It was here, on a small arm of the Caribbean located near the border of Panama and Colombia, that Encisco founded Santa Maria de la Antigua del Darién. The community became the first successful European settlement on the American mainland. The town flourished and for the next nine years it was a major center for Spanish exploration within the region.

In 1511, Vasco Nuñez de Balboa moved to Santa Maria de la Antigua del Darién, commonly called Antigua. When he arrived, he was told by the natives in the area that the isthmus had another coast and there was a great sea on the other side. On September 1, 1513, Balboa and his crew set out to trek through the dense rain forest to cross Panama. They journeyed in search of the vast body of water about which they had heard. Along the way, they had many skirmishes with local Amerindians and killed hundreds of them. After several weeks of travel, they reached a peak from which a vast expanse of ocean spread out before them. Balboa claimed the sea for Spain. Because the crew took a southward route from Antigua, they called the body of water the "South Sea." Later, of course, it would be renamed, the "peaceful," or Pacific Ocean.

Balboa's success created many enemies, some of whom were powerful. A few years after returning to Antigua, the new governor, Pedro Arias de Ávila accused Balboa of treason against Spain. Francisco Pizarro, who some years later would become the conqueror of Peru and the mighty Inca Empire, arrested Balboa. Although there is ample evidence to suggest that he was framed, Balboa was convicted. In 1519, he and a number of his supporters were executed in a public beheading.

That same year, Pedro Arias de Ávila, more commonly known as Pedrarias, moved the capital from the Darién area to a fishing village on the Pacific coast. The village was called *Panama* by the natives, meaning "plenty of fish." Conditions along the south coast are slightly drier and the Spaniards thought the area was healthier than locations along the Caribbean. Also, natives living along the Pacific shores were less hostile than those along the northern coast. Although they were still warriors, they used different methods of fighting than did the Darién natives and most other Caribbean coast tribes. For example, the western tribes did not use poisonous arrowheads. Physically they were much larger and stronger than natives living in the northern portion of the territory. Additionally, their settlement was in villages rather than in scattered dwellings.

SPANISH COLONIAL PERIOD

For nearly 300 years—from 1538 to 1821—Panama served as a strategic region of the vast Spanish Empire. The Spaniards made profitable use of the isthmus by using the area as a primary crossroad. It served as a vital link for transporting valuable goods between Spain and its colonies in the New World that faced the Pacific, such as Peru. People used the crossing, and Incan gold and silver as well as essential supplies, were marketed and shipped through Panama. The route used to transport these goods became known as the Camino Real, or Royal Road.

Toward the end of the seventeenth century, Panama's significance was beginning to decrease. Although the route was short, it proved to be labor intensive and expensive because of the constant loading and unloading of goods, followed by the difficult trek to the other coast. The route was also dangerous. Travelers were subject to periodic ferocious attacks from pirates and former African slaves who lived along the Camino Real.

INDEPENDENCE FROM SPAIN

Between 1808 and 1824, a "revolutionary fever" spread throughout the Spanish colonies in the area. Venezuela and Colombia

This Spanish fortress on the island of El Encanto in the Darién Gap was discovered by locals looking for buried treasure left by Spanish *conquistadors* (explorers). Once used as a thruway to transport loot, the Darién Gap is now about 100 miles of dangerous, undeveloped swampland and forest. Travel is done by dugout canoe or on foot.

broke away from Spanish rule in 1819, and together they united to form the Republic of Greater Colombia. Due to its remoteness, Panama tended to be unaffected by events happening elsewhere in Latin America.

Because Spain had shifted its gold shipping route to go around Cape Horn, the southern tip of the South American

continent, Panama's strategic and economic importance began to decline. Before long, the colony of Panama joined
others in the desire to be free of Spain's tight grasp. On November 28, 1821, Panama declared its independence from
Spain, then joined Simón Bolívar's Republic of Gran Colombia, which included Colombia, Venezuela, Ecuador, Peru, and
Bolivia. Panama was recognized as the Department of the
Isthmus. This relationship was rather short-lived, lasting only
a decade. When the confederation dissolved in 1830, Panama
became a province of New Granada, which later was renamed
Colombia. Although it was a turbulent relationship, it lasted
more than seven decades, until 1907.

CROSSING THE ISTHMUS BY RAIL

Soon after Balboa's epic crossing of the isthmus, the need for
some easy means of crossing Panama—a route linking the two
oceans—became apparent. In the early 1800s, both the United
States and France toyed with the idea of building a railroad
or cutting a canal through the country to make transoceanic
travel quicker. In 1835, President Andrew Jackson established
a commission to investigate the possibility of such a link. The
commission members decided that building a railway across
Panama would be the most efficient way to achieve this goal. As
a result, the United States immediately began negotiations with
the Republic of New Granada for the right to build a railroad
across the isthmus. It took the U. S. government 10 years to get
the plan moving forward. In 1846, Panama granted the right to
construct a transoceanic railroad.

In 1848 gold was discovered in California and by 1849
thousands of people began moving westward to seek their
fortunes. The urgency for building a railroad connecting the
eastern United States to the newly acquired west increased.
Construction of the railroad across Panama took five years and
thousands of people died. They were unable to withstand the

Building a railway across Panama ensured a more efficient building process for the upcoming canal project, and also provided faster access to the western United States for those traveling from the east to make their fortune in the Gold Rush. The U.S.-built railroad became the first transcontinental railway, stretching from Panama City to Colón.

oppressive heat and humidity of the tropical climate. Tropical diseases such as malaria and yellow fever also took a terrible toll. In addition to railroad rights, the United States was granted the power to intervene militarily to protect its new interest in New Granada.

Completed in 1855, the Panama Railway, which ran from Colón to Panama City, was the first transcontinental railroad in the Americas. There was a great rush to use the railroad, as it was a quick passage for people in search of fortune in the goldfields of California. This benefited the railway company, giving it a steady income from the onset of completion. In fact, within ten years, the Panama Railway was said to be the greatest revenue-earning property in the world. The success of the transcontinental railroad created even more urgency for building a canal through the country.

FREEDOM FROM COLOMBIA

While Panama was part of Colombia, the country experienced various conflicts with the government and its policies. This resulted again in multiple movements for independence, with the most successful campaign occurring under the direction of Tomás Herrera. In November 1840, during a civil war that had begun as a religious conflict, General Herrera declared Panama's independence from Colombia. After 13 months of freedom, the State of the Isthmus, as it was called, rejoined the Republic of New Granada.

For the next 60 years, Panama was in a state of almost constant turmoil. There was a seemingly endless turnover of governments and political leaders, resulting in considerable political and civil strife. Riots, rebellions, attempted secessions, and interventions by the United States were commonplace. This tumult would set the stage for a growing desire for an independent Panama.

Amid the political and civil strife were several specific situations that fed the growing appetite for independence. Throughout the mid- to late-nineteenth century, Panama experienced economic, political, and civil hardships. When the transisthmian railway was completed in 1855, linking the Atlantic and Pacific oceans, it inspired new hope in many Panamanian citizens. Panamanians became excited at the prospect of a canal through the country.

Finally, in the 1880s, a French company drafted a plan to build a canal across Panama. Shortly thereafter, however, it sold the rights to the plan to the United States. Because the United

States already had a dominant presence in Panama because of the railway, many Panamanians favored U.S. ownership of the canal. However, the Colombian government was not in favor of the proposed plan and therefore was slow in negotiations. Many Panamanians became increasingly frustrated with the government's slow responsiveness toward the canal. This, along with oppressive government policies, stirred the Panamanian desire for independence from Colombia.

With U.S. support, Panama declared its independence from Colombia on November 3, 1903. Within weeks, Panama sold the United States the rights to the canal. It gave the United States permission to dig the canal and to forever occupy the Canal Zone, a 10-mile-wide strip of land on either side of the waterway. The United States paid a price of $10 million, plus an annual $250,000 fee. Because the United States occupied the Canal Zone, Panama also granted the United States the right to interfere in Panama's affairs should it become necessary to protect the zone. This agreement, as one can imagine, would later cause controversy among many Panamanians.

STATUS AS A U.S. PROTECTORATE

From the very beginning of Panama's independence, the country was in a state of chaos, particularly political chaos. In 1904, the country became a protectorate of the United States, with a constitution that was very similar in many ways to that of the United States. The constitution called for a democratic, republic government, and the first elected president of the new nation was Manuel Amador Guerrero. The constitution also included a clause that gave the United States the right to impose in Panama's affairs to ensure order and to protect Panamanian sovereignty. As the United States was constructing the canal, it used the provision on various occasions, particularly during the years of 1908, 1912, and 1918. With the completion of the Panama Canal in 1920, the population experienced a period of rapid growth. Yet, the canal's completion did not calm the internal distaste that some Panamanians felt toward United States authority over the country.

Panama's protectorate status ended in 1939 by mutual agreement between both countries. This did not end the United States' direct involvement in the country, though, because it still had control over the Canal Zone. The change, however, did weaken the influence the United States wielded over the country.

BUILDING THE CANAL

Selecting a suitable route for a canal through Panama was not a simple choice. Much thought and deliberation went into choosing a proper site because many factors had to be considered. They included geographical (spatial) considerations, the geology of the area, and political and military concerns, among many.

As was mentioned, the French and the French Canal Company started the construction of the Panama Canal in 1880. Thousands of French workers died from exhaustion, heat stroke, and diseases. They were particularly susceptible to the dreaded malaria and yellow fever, which were carried by infectious mosquitoes. The French Canal Company eventually went bankrupt and sold the entire project to the United States for $40 million.

The Americans worked on the canal for 10 years, from 1904 to 1914. They, too, experienced the same problems as the French. The United States, however, had one major advantage over the French: a number of American medical doctors stationed in Cuba were working on treatments for both yellow fever and malaria. Even with the new treatments, which brought the diseases somewhat under control, thousands died while constructing the canal. Fortunately, the mortality rate was much lower than it had been for the French.

Finally, in 1914, the long-held dream of a canal linking the Atlantic and Pacific oceans became a reality. The canal was completed and open to marine traffic two years ahead of schedule.

Despite hiring the same man who oversaw the building of the Suez Canal in Egypt, the French failed to build a canal in Panama, and sold the rights to the United States government. The Colombian government's opposition to the United States led to Panama's declaration of independence from Colombia. Panama also granted to the United States rights to the canal and its surrounding area.

At the time and even today, it stands as one of history's greatest engineering and construction accomplishments.

PROTECTING THE CANAL

Protecting the Panama Canal required the strategic location of a number of U.S. military bases. Some of the military installations were in Panama, whereas others were scattered around the Caribbean Basin and the adjacent South American mainland. While the United States controlled the Canal Zone, American military units were a constant presence. Because the canal is a vital transportation route to the world, it needs to be defended. There was much controversy over the withdrawal of U.S. troops in 1999. Currently, concerns continue over the security of the Panama Canal, particularly from China and neighboring Colombia.

PETROLEUM PIPELINE

During the second half of the twentieth century, many ocean-going vessels, particularly supertankers that carry crude oil, were built that were too large to pass through the Panama Canal. As a result, a Trans-Panama pipeline was built in 1982, crossing the country near the Costa Rican border. Refineries from Alaska's North Slope, in particular, used the pipeline because it gave them a much shorter route to refineries in the Caribbean and along the Gulf Coast. Travel from Alaska, around the southern tip of South America, and on to refineries bordering the Gulf of Mexico in the southern United States could take up to 40 days. Using the pipeline, travel time was shortened to about 16 days, representing a huge savings in time and transportation costs. Yet, several factors caused the pipeline to close in 1996. Petroleum production began to decrease significantly in Alaska's North Slope, and oil production and refining in the western United States increased substantially. Also contributing to the pipeline's closure was the decision to allow Alaskan oil to be shipped outside of the United States, reducing the need and incentive for Alaskan oil to be shipped to the Gulf Coast.

NATIONALIZATION OF THE CANAL

In 1977, Panama and the United States agreed to gradually turn over the canal operations to Panama by the end of 1999. The Torrijos-Carter Treaty, signed by Panamanian military dictator General Omar Torrijos and U.S. former president Jimmy Carter, guaranteed the transfer of the canal and also neutrality in the Canal Zone. Signing of the treaty and the realization that they would finally own the canal was cause for great initial excitement among Panamanians. It did not take long, however, for reality to set in. As the deadline for the transfer approached, many people expressed deep concerns and reservations. At least some of their concerns were warranted. Today, a number of political, economic, and environmental problems have plagued Panama and its canal since the official transfer of ownership.

Although the Panama Canal still has significant value, traffic has been on a decline since 1970. Many of today's cargo ships are too large to navigate through the canal. In mid-2007, work began on an expansion of the Panama Canal and Panamanians look ahead once again to being one of the world's most important crossroads.

4

People
and Culture

People—their numbers, density, distribution, as well as their culture, or way of life, constitute the very heart and soul of any country. For this reason, many geographers regard population as being the single most important element of any nation. We will now investigate Panama's demographic conditions, or the major statistics that apply to its population. We will also touch briefly upon Panama's settlement patterns, where people live (or avoid) and why, as well as historical and present migrations. Finally, we will look briefly at major aspects of Panamanian culture, such as ethnic groups, language, and religion.

POPULATION

In early 2008, Panama's population is estimated to be approximately 3.25 million. This number is roughly comparable to that of

Connecticut, Iowa, or the Canadian province of Alberta. It also gives Panama the smallest population among all mainland Spanish-settled (or Portuguese-settled in the case of Brazil) countries.

The population is growing at an annual rate of natural increase (RNI) of about 1.5 percent (2007 est.), down from an explosive 3.3 percent in the 1970s. In Central America, only neighboring Costa Rica has a lower RNI. This shows tremendous progress during recent decades, reflected in greater prosperity and well-being. The figure of 1.5 percent gains additional meaning when it is compared to the annual gross domestic product (GDP). When the RNI is well below the GDP, it means that economic growth is outstripping population gains. In 2007 Panama's economy was growing at about 8 percent annually, a figure much higher than the country's yearly population increase. This will be discussed further in Chapter 6.

Another figure that shows great promise for the future is the total fertility rate (TFR). The TFR is the number of children to which the average woman will give birth during her childbearing years. In 2007, the figure stood at 2.66, less than half what it was three decades ago. In fact, the replacement rate is 2.1 (the .1 results from the fact that some women never bear children). In all of Central America, only Costa Rica has a lower TFR. By comparison, in Africa south of the Sahara, each woman will bear an average 5.6 children. The importance of this difference can be seen in the economic condition of the two regions. The per capita annual GDP south of the Sahara is about $1,200, whereas the figure is about $8,200 in Panama.

In other areas of demographic data, Panama compares favorably with many of the more-developed Latin American states. For example, about 30 percent of its population is under 15 years of age and 6.4 percent is 65 or older. This is much better than the age ratio in most less-developed countries (LDC). Birth rates (21.45/1,000 population) and death rates (5.44/1,000 population) are also favorable, much better than that of most

LDCs. In the 1970s, the average age was a very young 19 years. Today, it is 26.4 years. The significance of these figures, in terms of population growth, is that 19-year-olds are entering their childbearing years. Most 26-year-olds, on the other hand, have had and are now raising their children. This suggests that the rate of natural increase (RNI) will continue to drop.

Finally, perhaps the most significant indicator of a country's development and level of human well-being is life expectancy. Today, at birth, Panamanians can expect to live about 75.19 years (2007 data). Females average 77.8 years and males a somewhat shorter 72.69 years. Each of these figures is at least 10 years longer than the average life expectancy of the world's LDCs. Many conditions must be present if a country's people are to enjoy a long life expectancy. They include the eradication of diseases, good hygiene, a clean domestic water supply, and good health care.

SETTLEMENT

Settlement refers to where people live. Are they rural or urban? Is the population clustered or dispersed? Is the density high or low? Once geographers know these conditions, they can seek answers that will explain why such settlement patterns exist. Sometimes, the answer is found in what the authors call "too lands." These are places that are too hot, too cold, too wet, too dry, too rugged, too disease ridden, or too remote for people to live comfortably. The conditions also may impose difficulties for certain kinds of economic activities, such as farming or tourism. As you will see, Panama has some very interesting distributions and patterns of settlement and also its share of "too lands."

Panama's population density is 44 people per square mile (17 per square kilometer). This is far below the world average of 127 per square mile (49 per square kilometer). But such figures are all but useless to the geographer. They tell us very little about where the people actually live. Think of Egypt, for example. It has a density of 190 people per square mile (73 per square kilometer), but more than 90 percent of the people live in the narrow Nile Valley and Delta region, less than 10 percent of the country's total territory! To a lesser degree, Panama is somewhat similar to Egypt. Its population is extremely clustered.

Two of every three Panamanians live in an urban setting. In fact, about 90 percent of the population lives in the western half of the country, with nearly half of the country's people living in Panama City, Colón, or elsewhere in the immediate vicinity of these cities and the canal. To the east, there are no large communities and very few rural residents. Here the population is small and widely scattered. In addition, if a line was drawn dividing Panama in half, with Atlantic and Pacific territories, about 80 percent of the population would live on the Pacific side. Other than Colón, there are no major population clusters on the Atlantic side of the country.

Data such as these beg explanation. The very low population density of the eastern half and the Atlantic side of Panama can be explained by an inhospitable natural environment. Conditions are extremely hot, humid, and wet. Nearly impenetrable tropical highlands and soggy lowland marshes and swamps are widespread. Tropical diseases still pose a threat to residents of these areas. Because of the difficult environmental conditions, transportation linkages are poor to nonexistent throughout most of the region. The Darién Gap—the inhospitable environment of far eastern Panama and adjacent portions of Colombia—is impassable by vehicle. It is the only break, or gap, in the Pan-American Highway that extends from the Arctic shores of North America to the southern tip of South America. Approximately 53 percent of Panama's territory remains relatively untouched by human settlement or activity.

The natural environment also plays an important role as to where people live. In Chapter 2, you learned about orographic precipitation. The prevailing northeast trade winds

After a pirate attack left Panama City in ruins, the residents settled a few miles away and rebuilt their capital, beginning with Casco Viejo. The neighborhood, seen in this photo, still exists in Panama City as one of its old colonial districts and is a tourist attraction.

drop most of their moisture on the Caribbean-facing slopes of Panama's mountain backbone. As winds descend on the leeward (Pacific) side of the mountains, they become drier, creating rain-shadow conditions. That part of the western half of Panama south of the highlands, in particular, is drier. With drier conditions weather is more comfortable and soils are less leached, hence, more fertile. With less standing surface water, transportation routes are easier to build and maintain. And tropical diseases pose less of a threat.

URBAN CENTERS

Panama has three major cities: Panama City, Colón, and David, and a handful of smaller urban centers. The largest and most important is Panama City. The city proper is home to about 750,000 people, but the metropolitan area (the city, its surrounding suburbs, and the neighboring communities) has a population estimated to be nearly 1.25 million. Like many other large Latin American capitals, it is what geographers call a *primate city*. To qualify for this distinction, an urban center must be a country's largest city by a wide margin. Additionally, it must be the capital, as well as the country's leading economic and cultural center. Panama City qualifies in all these categories.

Located at the south entrance to the Panama Canal, Panama City's economy and population growth is booming. Fortunately, its economic and urban growth is not dependent solely upon the canal. It has a very diverse economic base and is rapidly becoming an important regional center for various services. In 2003, Panama City shared the honor of being named the "American Capital of Culture" with Curitiba, Brazil.

Colón, traditionally known as Panama's second city, has a population of about 210,000 people. Located at the north end of the Panama Canal, it is Panama's major port on the Atlantic Ocean. Within the last few decades, the city's economy and population has been in decline, and the city has fallen on hard times. Many people, particularly members of the elite and upper class and various European and Asian ethnic groups, have left the city. Some have moved across the isthmus to Panama City, and others have left the country. Today, most of the city's residents are of African descent, or *mestizos* (mixed Amerindian and European ancestry).

David is Panama's third-largest urban center, with about 125,000 residents. It is located in the far western part of the country, near the Costa Rican border. David is a thriving regional economic center that is located on the Pan-American Highway. Major economic activities include farming, ranching, and manufacturing. It also has a fairly well-developed tourist industry. Other than Panama City, David is Panama's most prosperous community.

The building of the Panama Canal and the railway expanded the local economy in Colón, which became the second-largest city in Panama. While a free trade zone has been established in Colón for importing and exporting purposes, shifting governments and populations have caused a serious decline in the city.

MIGRATION

Panama has experienced a "boom-and-bust" pattern of migration. During construction of the transisthmian railroad and canal, tens of thousands of people migrated to Panama in search of work. Many came from the West Indies, an immigration pattern that contributed the country's present-day black population. During periods of political instability or economic downturn, population decreased as many Panamanians became discouraged and left the country. Currently, emigration (leaving) and immigration (moving into) are nearly in balance. With work underway on enlarging the canal and the economy of Panama City booming, it is anticipated that the country will attract thousands of additional immigrants during the coming years.

During the past century, several significant migrations have occurred within Panama. For decades, many people moved in search of rural land on which to settle. This type of movement was particularly prevalent among traditional folk societies that practiced shifting, subsistence cultivation. With the building of the railroad and canal, internal migration from rural areas to Panama City and the surrounding communities increased, and the rural-to-urban pattern of migration continues today. Particularly, rural youth are attracted to the cities in hope of finding better jobs, education, government services, and even a little more excitement.

ETHNICITY

When Spaniards first arrived in what is now known as Panama, they found that the area was inhabited by various tribes of indigenous peoples. The Iberians (people from Portugal and Spain) simply added to the racial and cultural mix. Shortly after, Africans arrived, brought to the Spanish colony as slaves. With the construction of the railway and the canal in the nineteenth and twentieth centuries, Caribbean blacks and Chinese came to the isthmus to work as paid laborers. Blacks were considered the strongest laborers because they were accustomed to the tropical climate. Throughout the twentieth century, immigrants arrived from all over the world, especially the Americas, Europe, and Asia, attracted by the economic opportunities the projects provided. Panama's highly diverse society is descended

The transcontinental railway and the opening of the canal brought different people to Panama, including about 1,600 Chinese laborers. Those that stayed and established families contributed to Panama's Chinese community, which is the largest in Central America.

from natives and immigrants who, over a span of centuries, made Panama a melting pot of races and cultures.

About 70 percent of the population are mestizo, those descended from Europeans and Native Americans, or *mulattoes*, people of European and African heritage. Blacks, mostly from the West Indies, make up the second largest segment of the population, at 15 percent. About 10 percent of the population are white, primarily from the Iberian Peninsula. About 6 percent are Amerindian. There is a sizable minority of Jews, the sixth largest in all of Latin America including the Caribbean islands. Another one percent is Chinese, French, Greek, Italian, or Middle Eastern. Of Panama's indigenous Amerindian peoples, the Guaymi are the largest group. They are clustered in the western provinces. The Kuna are the second largest. They live in the Archipiélago de San Blas and on the nearby low-lying coastal plain. The Chocó live mainly in eastern Panama, in the Darién region near the border with Colombia.

LANGUAGE

Spanish, Panama's official language, is spoken by nearly everyone. Many Panamanians are bilingual, speaking Spanish and one other language. As a result of strong U.S. presence, about 14 percent of the population speaks English as its first tongue. Most business leaders and other professionals also speak English. Most blacks, particularly those along the northern coast and in Colón, speak a form of Creole English. Creole language incorporates English words, meanings, and grammar that are mixed with a number of other tongues as well.

There are also a number of Amerindian languages spoken. In fact, Panama is home to 14 native tongues, all of which are living, or spoken today, if even by small groups. Major languages and their estimated number of speakers are as follow:

Spanish	2,100,000
English (including Creole)	268,000
Ngäbere	128,000
Kuna	58,000
Chinese (various)	9,000
Buglere	2,500
Woun Meu	3,000
Emberá	700

Through time, the number of native language speakers has declined, while the number of Spanish speakers has increased. Changes of this nature are expected as a society undergoes the transition from folk to popular culture. Accepting the language of the dominant social, political, and economic group is the key to acceptance, and, therefore, success.

RELIGION

Roman Catholic priests arrived with the earliest Spanish colonists and were quite successful in their missionary effort to convert native peoples to their faith. Although the country does not have an official religion, about 80 percent of the population is Roman Catholic. This figure, however, can be somewhat misleading. Today, few people attend church services regularly. There is an often-heard Panamanian saying: "a good Catholic attends church three times—his or her baptism, marriage, and funeral." In reality, many people who rarely attend church do attend services on special holidays like Easter and Christmas. Some nominal Catholics practice Santería, a *syncretic* religion. A syncretic faith is one that blends elements of two or more religions into a combined belief system. Santería is a mix of Roman Catholic practices with various West African beliefs.

Protestants account for about 12 percent of the population. Their numbers have grown substantially during the last half of the twentieth century. Nearly all blacks, particularly those from the Caribbean, have a long-standing tradition of Protestantism. Other faiths include: Islam, (4.4%); Bahá'í, (1.2%); Buddhism, (1%); Judaism, (0.4%); Hinduism, (0.3%); and Greek Orthodox, (0.1%). The diversity of religions is further evidence of Panama's ethnic mix. Members of minority faiths have risen to positions of influence and power, including the country's president.

Culture, of course, includes all things that people do because they are human. Combined, these traits create the different ways of life that we recognize when studying the world's different cultural groups. Some important aspects of Panamanian culture are discussed in Chapter 6.

When Panama gained independence from Colombia, the government's constitution resembled the American one. Along with granting their citizens freedom of religion, the constitution also recognizes the Roman Catholic faith to be dominant in Panama. The religion is so widespread, there is a church in almost every town in Panama.

CHAPTER

5

Government and Economy

In Panama, the government's and the country's economy are very closely linked because of the canal and its importance. For this reason, government and economics have been combined into one chapter. From the dawn of the Spanish colonial era until the present day, Panama's political situation has been strongly influenced by its role as a "crossroad." To the earliest Spanish colonists, the narrow isthmus served as a bridge between the Atlantic and Pacific oceans. The isthmus served as the shortest route between the Spanish-held possessions in the Caribbean and their colonies along the Pacific coast of the Americas. During the nineteenth century, both the French and Americans also saw Panama as a crossroad, first spanned by rail and later by canal. The country's independence from Colombia also was closely linked to the planned building of a transisthmian canal. With these various developments, Panama's political fortunes became even more closely tied to foreign interests, hence, outside political influences. Not until the dawn of the twenty-first century was the country in a position to control both its own political destiny and management of the Panama Canal. And in terms of employment, income, and the country's economic well-being, the Panama Canal looms very large. It is the revenue-producing giant that towers above all other individual contributors to the country's economic well-being.

PANAMA'S GOVERNMENT

From the time the Spaniards discovered Panama, other countries have had a great influence on the way of life, including government and economy, throughout the country. For some 300 years, the Spanish traversed and ruled the isthmus. Governors of the territories were appointed, cities were founded, and trade routes were established, all under Spain's direction. Beginning in the early 1700s, the Spanish found other routes for shipment across the seas. This resulted in a sharp decline in the activity and influence of rulers throughout the isthmus. When other countries in Latin America, such as Venezuela and Colombia, were freed from Spanish rule, Panama seized upon the opportunity to join them. In 1821, Panama joined the federation known as the Republic of Greater Colombia. Panama remained a part of Colombia for over 50 years. During these years, there were several secessionist movements. Some were more successful than others. The most successful movement took place in 1840. Led by Tomás Herrera, Panama maintained an independent status for 13 months.

During the mid-nineteenth century, the United States saw both a need and an opportunity to develop Panama as a crossroad. When gold was discovered in California in 1848, concession was granted to the United States to build a railroad across the isthmus. After the railroad was completed in 1855, the presence of U.S. troops became more recurrent. At various times, even while Panama was still part of Colombia, the United States would send the Marines to ensure stability within the region. Reasons for a U.S. military presence varied from time to time. The primary concern, however, was always a perceived need to protect the United States-owned railway company, or other American interests in the isthmus. Although the railroad across the isthmus greatly reduced the transportation time between the oceans, it involved time-consuming and costly transshipment. Goods had to be offloaded from ships, placed on or in railcars, and then again offloaded from the railroad and loaded onto ships. The United States wanted to build a faster route, by water, that would not involve the transshipping of cargo. The Colombian government, however, balked. It would not allow the United States to build a waterway through the isthmus that was still a portion of Colombia. When Panama revolted against Colombia in 1903, the United States supported its actions. Once again, the U.S. military intervened. Naval vessels were dispatched to protect Panama from Colombia. On November 3, 1903, Panama became the last of the mainland Latin American republics to achieve independence. (Belize and the Guianas, which gained independence much later, are not considered to be part of Latin America.)

POLITICAL TURBULENCE

Since Panama's independence from Colombia in 1903, the country has experienced various degrees of political turbulence. At different times, the country has undergone United States intervention, suffered under an oligarchy, and been in the clutches of a tightfisted dictatorship. Each of these events has been cause for political turmoil at different times in Panama.

As noted previously, the United States presence in Panama began decades before the country's independence. United States military forces were often sent to the isthmus to oversee and protect matters regarding the railroad. After Panama declared its

Relations between the United States and Panama became strained as the Panamanian government demanded more control of the region and less American involvement. In 1964, protests and riots continued until President Lyndon B. Johnson restored diplomatic ties and began to negotiate for a new treaty with Panamanian president Robert Chiari.

independence, the Hay-Bunau-Varilla treaty was negotiated for the building of the canal. Once this was done, U.S. troops became a permanent presence in Panama. This presence, as you might assume, created considerable tension between the United States and many Panamanians. It was felt that the United States intervened in matters not defined in previous treaty agreements and amendments. Some members of Panama's elite, and particularly those involved in or supporting the country's oligarchy, supported the U.S. presence. Oftentimes, they would even request the intervention of U.S. forces to control and regulate popular protests and revolts.

For several decades after Panama gained its independence, the United States supervised the country's national elections. It was not only during elections, however, that riots took place. Resentment towards a continuous U.S. presence grew. This anger, alone, accounted for many uprisings throughout the country, particularly those during the 1960s. In 1977, during the administration of U.S. former president Jimmy Carter and Panamanian military strongman General Omar Torrijos, the landmark Panama Canal treaties were signed. These agreements slowly transferred rights and control of the canal from the United States to Panama. After the treaties were enacted, relations between Panama and the United States significantly improved. And for a few years, Panama would remain a stable country.

Turmoil in Panama picked up again in the early 1980s. No longer was an oligarchy ruling over Panama. Instead, a dictatorship held the country in its grasp for six years, from 1983 until 1989. General Manuel Noriega took control of the Panama Defense Forces (PDF) and the civilian government. In order to suppress opposition to his regime, Noriega created and installed the Dignity Battalions. The United States was familiar with Noriega. From the late 1950s until the early 1980s, he was a close ally of the United States'. Relations became increasingly intense, however, after he took control of Panama. Flames of conflict were fanned by allegations that he was friendly to, or actually working with, Communist countries. There were also deep suspicions that Noriega was involved in the trafficking of drugs.

Based upon the deteriorating relationship between the United States government and Panama's government under Noriega, the United States initiated plans to overthrow the Panama government. To accomplish this, the United States first imposed devastating economic sanctions and held back on military assistance. As a result, Panama experienced an economic crisis. In December of 1989, the United States invaded Panama. Restoring democracy by ending the dictatorship of Manuel Noriega was not the only reason for the invasion. To protect American lives, to defend the canal, and to stop drug trafficking were the other reasons the United States intervened. The invasion resulted in the capture of Noriega and an end to the oppressive regime.

After the United States invasion, $1 billion in U.S. aid was given to Panama to restore the country's economy. Although it took a few years for Panama to bounce back, the determined country eventually did so. (In 2007, Manuel Noriega was released from prison in the United States after serving his term. He was immediately extradited to France, where he is sentenced to serve a 10-year prison term. Panama also seeks to imprison Noriega on various charges.)

GOVERNMENT STRUCTURE

For more than 150 years, the United States exerted great influence on Panama. For more than a century, U.S. troops were stationed throughout the region. Their continuous presence influenced many aspects of Panamanian life, including the government. Panama, like the United States, has a representative democracy. This means that the citizens of Panama choose their officials to represent their opinions and concerns on governmental issues. Panama's government, like that of the United States, consists of three branches. Officials within the executive and legislative branches are elected by direct vote for five-year terms. The judiciary branch is an independently appointed sector. Currently, the legislative branch consists of a 78-member single chamber, or unicameral, National Assembly. The executive branch also consists of a president and two vice presidents. However, in 2004 the constitution was changed. The changes made, which include downsizing the National Assembly to 71 members and having only one vice president, will be implemented with national elections in 2009. The judicial branch of government is made up of a nine-member Supreme Court. All subordinate tribunals, municipal, and district courts are also included in the judiciary branch.

In addition to the three branches of government, there exist various other agencies that provide important services to Panama and its residents. One of these organizations is the Electoral Tribunal. Representatives from the legislative, executive, and judicial branches, along with three elected judges, comprise the committee. The duties of the Electoral Tribunal are extensive. Among the various responsibilities are to supervise voter registration, the election process, and the activities of the political parties. Also included is the task of interpreting the electoral laws.

Since Panama's independence, the country has had four constitutions. Prior to adoption of the current constitution, the previous ones were adopted in 1904, 1941, and 1946. Panama's present constitution was implemented on October 11, 1972. The various constitutions have differed considerably in the areas of influence that each of them emphasized. They have all been a reflection of the political circumstances existing at the time of their adoption. Instead of creating an entirely new governing document, the 1972 Constitution has been amended frequently. Major reforms were incorporated into the document in 1978, 1983, 1994, and most recently in 2004. When new constitutions were created rather easily, the public was more apt to lose confidence in the rule of law. It has been a challenge to the government to restore the confidence of Panama's citizens. Panama is made up of nine administrative provinces and three provincial-level territories, commonly called *comarcas*. The territories are home to large populations of indigenous people. Governors appointed by the president administer the provinces. As for the territories, leaders of the native groups negotiate directly with the national government.

RECENT TRENDS AND CONDITIONS

On December 31, 1999, the United States turned full control of the Panama Canal over to the Panama Canal Authority (ACP). For the first time in its history, Panama was in control of both its government and the canal. The transfer included the Canal Zone, a 10-mile wide (16-kilometer) strip extending five miles (8 kilometers) on each side of the canal. During the first decade of the twenty-first century, Panama has experienced an era of unparalleled stability in terms of both its economy and government. The government has vigorously marketed the country's various strengths to the global community. Tax and social security reforms have been implemented by the government to further enhance the economy and the well-being of the populace. Many important trade agreements were designed to foster economic growth. In December 2006, Panama and the United States negotiated a free trade agreement between the two countries. As construction on the expansion of the Panama Canal advances, the government of Panama will continue to develop its economy.

Panama's geographic location provides the country with many economic advantages. This is particularly true in regard to the booming services sector. A very significant component of this sector is the Panama Canal, which provides just over $1 billion in revenue to the country each year. The canal has contributed to Panama becoming a leader in international trading as well as an important maritime center. Historically, Panama has experienced a largely "boom-and-bust" economy marked by sharp fluctuations. Today, however, the country can boast of having one of Latin America's most vigorous economies, with an annual growth rate of about 8 percent. Investors from the United States and elsewhere have discovered the opportunities Panama has to offer. They are eagerly investing in a variety of new developments. With relatively pleasant tropical weather, few natural hazards, and many scenic views, the country provides a variety of attractive amenities. Even with a growing economy, however, many Panama residents have not seen the benefits. Panama has

After 85 years of United States control, Panama took full command of the Panama Canal on December 31, 1999. At a ceremony on the banks of the waterway on December 14, 1999, dignitaries from Spain, Latin America, and the United States watched as former president Jimmy Carter exchanged documents with Panamanian president Mireya Moscoso, completing a process he began in 1977.

a large disparity between socioeconomic classes and many residents live in poverty, even with present economic growth.

GENERAL ECONOMIC DATA

Many statistical data are readily available for the study of a country's economy. There are various figures for certain components of every country's gross domestic product (GDP), unemployment and inflation rates, and numbers for the distribution of wealth throughout the country. Panama's gross domestic product (GDP), or the value of all the goods and services it produces on an annual basis, is $26.16 billion (2006). The country's $8,200 per capita GDP-PPP is one of the highest in Latin America. The figure indicates GDP purchasing power parity, or how many goods and services that amount would purchase in the United States. This ranking places Panama in the category of an upper-middle-income country.

Despite the country's positive economic data, there remain causes for alarm. Nearly 35 percent of all Panamanians continue to live below the poverty line. About 8 percent of the population is unemployed and many more are underemployed. That is, they hold jobs that are low paying and from which they are unable to make an adequate living. As a result, there is a huge gap between the rich and the poor in Panama. The rich are very rich and live lives of considerable material comfort. The poor, meanwhile, are very poor. Panama ranks as one of the world's most unequal countries.

Such figures and conditions, however, must be viewed with some caution. Many Panamanians continue to practice a traditional folk culture. At the extreme, they live completely outside of the cash economy; rather, they are very self-sufficient and provide for themselves. In the context of their culture and its socioeconomic expectations, they may be quite successful and live comfortable lives. One must always remember that statistical data relating to economic conditions are measured by the rules of contemporary commercial societies.

Panama's imports exceed its exports by over $2.5 billion. Because the country generates much of its income from service-related industries, it tends to rely on imports for many goods. The country's major exports include bananas, petroleum products, shrimp, sugar, coffee, and clothing. It imports such products as capital goods, crude oil, food products, chemical, and other consumer goods.

Panama's geographic location has been a huge asset to the country's economy. It has been relatively easy (although incredibly costly) to establish an economy that is heavily based upon the provision of services. In fact, almost 80 percent of its GDP comes from the services sector. The Panama Canal and its activities, banking, insurance, the Colón Free Trade Zone, maritime activities, and other businesses are some of the services. The industry sector accounts for nearly 77 percent of the GDP, while agriculture is at an all time low of providing only 8 percent to the nation's economy.

PRIMARY INDUSTRIES

Primary industries are those that exploit natural resources and produce raw materials. For centuries, before Panama was used as a transit point, subsistence agricultural and farming practices were the dominant economic activities for the majority of Panamanians. Although not as abundant, agriculture and farming still play a role in the economy of Panama. The lumbering, mining, and fishing industries are also present and successful to various degrees throughout Panama today.

Farming

In 1998, less than 10 percent of Panama's land was considered arable, or suitable for farming. Of the available land, the best lands are in the hands of only a few farmers. Much of the country's land, more than half, is swampy or forested, hence, uncultivated. A small percent of the land is being used to pasture livestock, such as cattle and pigs. For years, raising livestock and growing crops were the country's primary economic activities. Today, however, the agricultural sector remains fairly underdeveloped. In fact, most farming practices tend to be primitive, which results in lower productivity and more intense labor. The agricultural techniques used, such as the traditional slash-and-burn shifting cultivation, tend to be somewhat destructive. They do not make proper use of the land. Studies have shown, for example, that the products produced by a natural tropical rain forest are of greater value than alternative uses of the land. The result of shifting cultivation is widespread shortage of farmland, resulting in ever-increasing conflicts among rural Panamanians.

One of Panama's major exports, coffee, is finding a place in specialty markets in Europe and in the United States as growers expand their business expertise. While some growers, like this woman, may still be forced to sell their crops to local coffee companies, others are finding a way to negotiate overseas contracts to market their coffee on an international level.

The agriculture sector of the economy employs approximately 20 percent of the labor force. However, much of the labor in this sector is engaged in subsistence farming. This results in a lower productivity level that inhibits the export of many agricultural goods. Some crops are grown on tropical plantations, most of which are clustered in the northwestern region of the country. Crops grown for export on plantations tend to be produced using more effective techniques and technology. Bananas, coffee, and sugar are the three primary crops grown for export. Other important crops include rice, corn, some vegetables, and various types of fruit.

Lumbering

Slightly more than half of Panama's land area is comprised of forests. However, up to 400 different tree species may occupy a single square mile, and the vast majority of them are softwoods, of little if any commercial value. Forests in the Darién and Bocas del Toro provinces do contain an abundance of valuable hardwood trees, the logs of which are much in demand and exported. Perhaps the best known and most valuable tropical wood harvested in the region is mahogany, which is prevalent in the Darién area.

Mining

Mining accounts for a very small portion of the country's GDP. Among the minerals extracted are manganese, iron ore, and gold. The only ore that Panama has in abundance is copper. Reserves mined in the western part of the country make Panama the world's ninth largest storehouse of this mineral.

Fishing

Facing two large bodies of water, the Pacific Ocean and the Caribbean Sea, Panama has an excellent outlet to fish and other marine resources. Freshwater fishing is available in the Chiriqui River and several other streams. Deep sea fishing—both commercial and sport—is popular along the Pacific and Caribbean coasts. In the Pacific, shrimp and prawns are the primary catch. During recent years, shrimp farms have become increasingly popular. In fact, a large portion of Panama's exported shrimp are now raised on shrimp farms.

SECONDARY INDUSTRIES

Whereas primary industries produce products in their most natural forms—mining the ore, cutting the timber, harvesting marine life, or raising crops—secondary industries alter the materials. This is done by either changing their form, or combining them with some other material to produce more valuable commodities. The change can be something simple, such as making a handicraft product like pottery or woven fabrics, or it can be more complex, such as manufacturing electronic products or machinery. About 18 percent of Panama's labor force is engaged in manufacturing. Yet secondary industries contribute only about 16.5 percent of the country's GDP.

Manufacturing

A wide variety of products are manufactured in Panama. Among the leading industries are food processing, brewing, and oil refining. Most of the manufacturing, however, is intended either to support local construction industries or domestic markets for consumer goods. Products manufactured for such purposes include fabricated metal, petroleum products, and building materials for the construction sector. Primary goods produced for consumers include paper and paper products, household goods, processed foods and beverages, and clothing.

Energy Production

Just over half of Panama's electricity requirements are generated from hydroelectric power. The power comes from dams built on Lake Bayano, Lake Alajuela, and a few smaller dams.

The rest of Panama's energy is supplied from imported petroleum. Although Panama is not known for exporting energy, the country does have an indirect role in the world's energy market. A large number of oil shipments pass through the Panama Canal each year. Petroleum, in fact, is one of the primary commodities that is shipped through the canal. Ironically, a major reason for the current work to enlarge the canal is that the existing canal can no longer accommodate today's huge oil tankers. A great deal of coal also passes through the canal.

TERTIARY INDUSTRIES

Tertiary activities are those that provide services to the primary and secondary divisions. In addition to aiding the other sectors, these activities also provide goods and service to the general public. They are typical of a postindustrial economy.

Panama's economy is based primarily on the services sector. Major contributors include the Panama Canal, banking, business, and insurance. It also involves the Colón Free Zone, education- and health-related activities, law enforcement, entertainment, and tourism. In fact, the well-developed services industry accounts for nearly 80 percent of the country's GDP, and employs almost 70 percent of the labor force. The Panama Canal alone accounts for roughly 10 percent of the country's GDP. Other areas in the services sector of Panama's economy are continuing to develop. Some areas that are showing considerable growth include international banking, maritime services, tourism, and shipping.

The Colón Free Zone (CFZ) was established in 1953 at the Caribbean gateway to the Panama Canal. Commercial activity that develops in this trade center has an enormously positive effect on Panama's economy. Housing more than 1,500 companies, the CFZ is the largest free trade zone in the Western Hemisphere. Its primary advantage is that companies can import goods free from duties, tariffs, or most other forms of taxation. Goods are supplied to the CFZ from all over the world. Most imports, however, come from the Far East, with China being the largest supplier. Colombia is the largest single buyer of the merchandise. Combined, the United States, Canada, and various Latin American countries buy over 80 percent of all the exports from the CFZ. This center of trade plays a major role in the economy of Panama.

Panama's financial sector started to develop in 1970 when a law was passed that allowed secret bank accounts and favorable terms of taxation. Panama houses state banks, locally registered banks, and international, or offshore, banks. While the local banks conduct most of their operations in Panama, the international banks emphasize business with foreign clients. With more than 100 banks operating, the banking industry provides 10,000 well-paid jobs.

One area of the service sector that really has started to expand during recent years is call centers. In 2003, call centers employed over 300,000 people, a number that is expected to more than double by 2008. Panama is an ideal location for call centers for various reasons. First, many residents are bilingual and can speak both English and Spanish. Also in 2001, the Panamanian government enacted a law to lower the taxes on all calls. As a result, the number of people employed by call centers tripled within a short period of time. Finally, Panama is both politically and economically stable. These factors make Panama an ideal location for call centers supporting a variety of companies from all over the world.

Panama is an attractive place to visit that offers many amenities and attractions. The country can offer the canal, traditional cultures, and modern cities, and many cultural events and sites. It has beautiful landscapes, world-class beaches, dense tropical rain forests, and abundant wildlife. Thus, each year, more and more people choose Panama as a vacation destination. The Panamanian government has been promoting the fact that Panama City is the only city in the world with a tropical

With lush natural resources attracting people from all over the world, Panama has taken steps to preserve its environment while encouraging the growth of tourism. The government has established 14 national parks, which cover 29 percent of the country, where visitors can participate in various outdoor activities, including hiking, bird watching, and diving.

rain forest within its city limits. Many commercial cruise ships travel to and through the Panama Canal. There also are one-day boat rides that take tourists through the canal.

Due to its pleasant climate, Panama is becoming an attractive retirement center. It uses the U.S. dollar and many people speak English. These are but a few advantages that have attracted a rapidly increasing number of retirees to the country in recent years.

TRANSPORTATION

The Panama Canal plays a significant role in Panama's economy. On a local scale, it provides Panama with income and thousands of jobs. Internationally, the canal plays a central role in world trade. Four percent of world trade passes through the canal and up to 14,000 ships pass through annually. In recent years, the canal has brought in slightly over $1 billion in annual revenue. Each year, canal traffic continues to increase.

Ships continue to be built larger and larger. In fact, in the 1960s, some oil supertankers were too large to pass through the canal. The trip around the Horn (the southern tip of South America) adds about 8,000 miles (12,900 kilometers) to a journey between the east and west coasts of the United States. Huge container ships now carry a tremendous amount of cargo from eastern Asia to the United States Atlantic ports. For those unable to pass through the canal, an extra 5,000 miles (8,000 kilometers) is added to the voyage. The actual distance saved by using the Panama Canal varies depending on where the cargo is coming from and its destination. Through less fuel consumption and fewer maintenance repairs to the ships, more than $100,000 is saved per vessel by making passage through the canal, rather than rounding the Horn. By using the canal, the ships save time, which consequently leaves them available to haul more shipments. This makes the vessels more profitable for the companies.

To keep up with the demand, Panama started to consider options to expand the size of the current canal. After much deliberation, the government approved a $5.2 billion project to expand the Panama Canal. Work began on the enlargement in September 2007 and is expected to be completed in 2014 or 2015. With the construction of a new set of locks, the expansion will build a new lane of traffic following the existing canal route. These locks will also double the canal's traffic capacity by allowing more vessels to pass through and will accommodate much longer and wider ships. When the expansion is complete, the canal will allow ships double the size of the current *Panamax*, or maximum length of a ship able to transit the canal, to pass through. With the addition of the larger ships to those already passing through the canal each year, traffic is expected to reach 17,000 ships annually.

The canal's expansion will benefit the local economy as well as shipping industries across the world. With more ships being able to pass through the canal, the amount of goods that can pass through will increase dramatically, and more tolls will be paid, which will generate more income for Panama. Martin Torrijos, Panama's president, projected that the expanded canal will generate enough capital to turn Panama into a first-world country. Although the project is expensive for Panama, it is expected to bring in $6 billion by 2025.

Currently, the canal employs roughly 8,000 workers. With the expansion, some 40,000 new jobs are expected to be created, many of which are to be filled by Panamanians. This should boost the economy by lowering the percentage of unemployed residents. After the canal expansion is completed, more jobs will again be created since more workers will be needed to keep up with the increase in cargo.

THE PIPELINE

As oil tankers started to become larger, they could no longer pass through the canal. In the early 1980s, a pipeline was built to move petroleum across the isthmus, rather than around Cape Horn. Its primary role was to transfer crude oil from Alaska's North Slope to refineries on the U.S. Gulf Coast. When Alaskan production started to fall, shipments via the pipeline declined, consequently resulting in the facility being shut down. From 1982 to April 1996, however, the 81-mile (131 kilometers)-long pipeline transported almost 3 billion barrels of crude oil.

In June 2003, the owner of the Trans-Panama pipeline, Petroterminal de Panama, reopened the pipeline. Their primary customer is Ecuadorian crude oil that is transported from the Pacific to a Caribbean port that will further distribute the oil to refineries in the region.

THE PAN-AMERICAN HIGHWAY

The Pan-American Highway is actually a group of roads that unofficially link Alaska's Prudhoe Bay on the Arctic Ocean to the southernmost tip of South America. There is, however, one stretch of 54 miles (87 kilometers) through which no road exists. This area is called the Darién Gap, a region of extremely dense rain forest, nearly impenetrable uplands, and the vast swampy lowland of Colombia's Atrato River. Currently, an all-weather highway extends as far east as Yaviza in Panama. One plan calls for the highway to be extended from there, across the low Serranía del Darién, to the Gulf of Urabá. Transit across the gulf would be by ferry to an as yet undecided destination in Colombia (but one currently reached by a year-round highway).

PANAMA IN THE GLOBAL ECONOMY

Despite its size, Panama plays an influential role in the global economy, which can be attributed to the Panama Canal. The expansion of the canal will have a significant impact on Panama's role in the global economy. Also attributing to Panama's role in world trade is the Colón Free Trade Zone. It is the largest free trade zone in the Western Hemisphere and one of the largest in the world. Thousands of merchants from all over the world conduct business with the trade center.

Events across the world affect Panama's economy. Panama is experiencing an economic boom and attracting global attention. The government has promoted the small country as a financial haven in a region formerly known for political and economic instability. Today, Panama has many exciting projects underway. Panama City, in particular, is booming with development and expansion. Other areas of the country are prospering as well, with refinery, port, and other projects. Panama's economic future appears to be positive.

6

Living in Panama Today

F or many Panamanians, life has never been better. Signs of hope, optimism, and prosperity are evident throughout the country and at all social and economic levels. Statistics provide evidence of this newfound level of well-being. In this chapter, you will get a glimpse of life in Panama today. How well-off are Panamanians? What do they do? What are they like? These are just some of the questions that will be answered as you journey through contemporary Panama.

HUMAN DEVELOPMENT

Since 1990 the United Nations Development Program has published a Human Development Index (HDI) ranking the world's countries. This ranking is perhaps the single most valid source of informa-tion showing how well-off people are in various nations. Positions in the HDI ranking are based on three criteria: health, knowledge, and standard of living. Panama ranks fifty-eighth among the 177 countries that appear in the HDI listing. This places the country in sixth place among the 20 mainland Latin American nations. Only Argentina (ranked thirty-sixth, the highest position among mainland Latin American states), Chile, Uruguay, Costa Rica, and Mexico place higher than Panama. Of greatest importance, however is the fact that Panama steadily improved its position in the rankings since the country first appeared on the index.

When looking over the HDI, two things stand out: economic development and political stability. It becomes evident that a stable economy and a responsible government that is sensitive to people's needs go hand in hand. In fact, all of the criteria used in the rankings are closely linked. The turbulence and corruption that were earmarks of Panama's government for decades have somewhat subsided. This, in turn, has encouraged economic growth. A stronger economy supports such things as improvements in education, better medical facilities and health care, and the building of an improved infrastructure. These developments create a higher standard of living.

A CULTURAL TRANSITION

Many Latin Americans, including Panamanians, are undergoing a very important cultural transition. They are turning away from the traditional ways of life that their ancestors practiced for centuries. It is a life journey that can be very difficult and painful for many who are undergoing these changes.

Geographers refer to the "old time" ways of traditional living as *folk culture*. Within a folk culture, people tend to be self-sufficient; they rely on themselves, rather than others, to provide their needs. Their economy is simple; they raise, hunt, gather, build, or make those things that they need. What they are unable to provide for themselves, they acquire through simple barter, or trade. Their learning is from observation and experience, rather than the classroom and formal schooling.

As a result, most folk are illiterate. They often live in remote rural areas. There, they are isolated from new ideas, modern material objects and their use, and the helter-skelter fast pace of modern urban living. Change is often seen as threatening; they are conservative and work steadfastly to maintain the status quo. Their worldview rarely extends beyond the limits of their known local surroundings.

With urbanization and modernization come many changes in a people's way of life. Societies that live a fast-paced, outward looking, rapidly changing lifestyle are said to practice a popular culture. Individuals are highly specialized in what they know and are able to do; hence, they must rely upon others for nearly all of their needs. In order to obtain these necessities, whether material goods or services, they must pay cash. In doing so, their economy changes from simple barter to an often confusing monetary system. To live and compete successfully in popular culture, one must be literate in terms of both reading and writing, and also mathematics. New ideas, materials, and challenges come at a blindingly fast pace. Rather than being threatened by change, people immersed in a popular culture thrive on trends, fads, variety, and anything new. Their world view also is outward and global in scope.

This is the transition that many Panamanians are making today. Whether Amerindian, African, or European in ancestry, the past century has brought about many huge changes in the way of life experienced by Panama's people. The transition from folk to popular culture is ongoing today. Data suggest that perhaps 10 percent of the population still remains very traditional, with another perhaps 25 percent of the population still undergoing the transition between traditional and modern living. Statistical data provide several clues. For example, about 8 percent of Panamanians remain illiterate (although certainly many more possess only a limited ability to read and write). Six percent of the population is Amerindian, but many more are mestizo or mulatto. Many of these Panamanians continue to

The development of tourism and transportation throughout Panama has threatened the cultural preservation and tribal independence of its indigenous people. Rodrigo Hernandez, one of the leaders of the Kuna Indians, is working with other tribal leaders to balance the influx of modern industry with his tribe's traditions and customs.

practice a traditional folk way of life. Perhaps the single most important clue is found in agriculture. About 21 percent of all Panamanians are engaged in farming, but agriculture only contributes about 7 percent of the country's gross domestic product. This suggests that many farming people practice subsistence, rather than commercial, farming. Nearly all such individuals continue to follow traditional folkways.

Finally, about one-third of the country's population is rural, also a characteristic folk trait.

Today's Panamanians can be found at both ends of the cultural spectrum. Some continue to practice very traditional ways of living much as did their ancestors many generations ago. Others, however, are every bit as modern and "advanced" as you and I in their way of living. Most Panamanians are someplace in between the two extremes. Stop for a minute to think what it must be like to make the jump between folk and popular culture! What problems would an individual or family face in leaving their traditional way of living and trying to adapt to a new, fast-paced, city lifestyle? Your answers will help you better understand the challenge facing many Panamanians today.

SOCIAL CONDITIONS

Panamanian society is not rigidly structured. There is a small upper class called Creoles, who are mostly urban. Many of the elite are of European descent, although there are Americans, Italians, Jews, Chinese, Arabs, and others. The middle class is substantial and includes individuals of all races and ethnic groups. The middle class also mainly live in urban areas. They hold jobs as shopkeepers and other businesses-related activities, are professionals in education or healthcare, or are providers of government and other services. A small group, composed mainly of people who continue to practice a traditional folk culture, fall within the lower socioeconomic class. Most members of this group are rural and of Amerindian, black, or mixed ancestry.

Human rights and equality have only been constitutionally safeguarded in Panama since 2001. Today, discrimination continues to exist against women, Amerindians, blacks, and other ethnic minorities. Nonetheless, individuals of any race or ethnicity can earn social acceptance, even within the upper class. Upward mobility is based upon such factors as education, communication skills (including accent), proper dress, manners, and other aspects of behavior. Many women hold top positions, particularly in education and government service. In fact, a woman—Mireya Moscoso Rodríguez–served as the country's president from 1999 to 2004. Nonetheless, relations between males and females remain stereotypically Latin. Many males

President Mireya Moscoso Rodríguez (1999–2004) brought about a change in Panamanian politics when she took office as the first female president in the country's history. Her ascent to political success is a symbol of the social equality women in Panama have worked hard for over the years.

continue to exhibit traits of *machismo,* an exaggerated sense of masculinity or virility. Violence against women continues to be a serious problem in the country.

Except in urban slums, crime is quite scarce. Even in large cities like Colón and Panama City where robberies are rather common and drug smuggling and trading exists, more serious crimes are rare, unlike many other Latin American countries. Also, unlike many of its neighbors, Panama has not suffered from leftist guerrilla movements and devastating civil conflict.

FOODWAYS

When you think about Latin American food, what comes to mind? For many Northern Americans, the answer would be spicy hot dishes featuring staples such as maize (corn), beans, tomatoes, and tortillas. If you travel to Panama expecting to find cuisine similar to "Mexican food" in the United States, you would be greatly disappointed! Some dishes may be spicy, but little if any of the food eaten by Panamanians resembles the TexMex diet with which we are familiar.

The greatest differences in Panamanians' diets are found between the rural *campesino* families, who are still immersed in a traditional folk culture, and contemporary urbanites. One characteristic of a folk society, you will recall, is conservatism. Things rarely change and this certainly holds true for diets. Many traditional folk people eat basically the same thing day after day, year after year, throughout their lifetime. The ingredients, preparation, and serving change little if any. Some of us would find this kind of diet to be incredibly boring. In the cities, diets range from traditional to as varied as the North American diet. You will recall that change and variety are two key traits of popular culture, and this holds true for foods and beverages as well.

In Panama, there is a saying "If you haven't eaten rice, you haven't eaten." Rice is the staple foodstuff and is eaten daily in many households. It is often served with beans, fish or other seafood, beef or pork, or eggs. Vegetables and spices (some hot) may be added.

As elsewhere in Latin America, some corn is eaten, although it has never been the primary foodstuff in Panama. It appears in the form of cakes, tortillas, gruel (porridge), or as an ingredient in a soup or some other dish. Plantains (a bananalike fruit that must be cooked) are an important staple, particularly in the folk diet. They are roasted or boiled as a soup that may include some kind of meat and coconut. Vegetables and fruits are part of the main meal or eaten as a between-meal snack. Panama has many tropical fruits, such as papayas, mangoes, pineapples, and bananas. Most Panamanians drink coffee with their breakfast. Fruit drinks are popular among children, and beer and other alcoholic beverages are enjoyed among adults, particularly by males.

Some city people continue to enjoy a traditional diet. Most, however, enjoy a variety of international foods—including the fast foods with which Americans and Canadians are so familiar! Because of their great ethnic diversity, Panama City and Colón have a wide variety of restaurants featuring cuisine from around the world. And nearly all communities have at least one Chinese restaurant. Many rural families eat only two meals a day, a large breakfast and an early (for Latin America) dinner, served in the late afternoon or early evening. As is true in North America, dining patterns vary greatly among city dwellers. Some eat two meals a day, others three. Some eat a hearty breakfast and the dinner; others avoid breakfast and eat lunch.

HOLIDAYS AND ENTERTAINMENT

Panamanians celebrate a number of holidays. Some, such as Christmas, New Year's Day, and Easter are celebrated at the same time and in the same way as in the United States and Canada. Two independence days are celebrated in Panama: November 3 from Colombia and November 28 from Spain. Other holidays include Day of the Martyrs (January 9), Labor Day (May 1), and Mother's Day (second Sunday in December).

Such holidays are occasions for family gatherings, parades, feasts, and other appropriate activities. On religious holidays, many Panamanians attend church services. Most villages also hold celebrations honoring their patron saint. Some of the larger communities hold Sunday rodeos in which cowboys compete. Different racial and ethnic groups also have celebrations of their own. Many blacks, for example, celebrate the Congo, an event that honors their African heritage.

Carnaval is the most widely celebrated annual event. Much of the country closes down during the period from Saturday to Tuesday preceding Ash Wednesday. Celebrations are held

Combining modern trends and traditional customs, many Panamanians are bridging a cultural gap between folk and pop. Events such as the National Festival of the Mejorana in Guarare, seen here, help bolster national pride and cultural awareness by including musical presentations, folk dances and songs, bullfights, and folk art.

throughout the country and vary somewhat from place-to-place. In most locations, however, a king and/or queen is chosen, parades are held, and partying may go on around the clock.

As is true of all other aspects of culture, the primary differences in the way Panamanians entertain themselves exist between rural and urban dwellers. Folkways continue to be practiced by many rural people. Activities include a rich heritage of folk practices relating to music, dance, art, and games including sports. In the cities, on the other hand, entertainment differs little from that with which readers are familiar. Pop music (perhaps with a heavier Latin or Caribbean beat!) is very—well—popular! The names of popular international singers are widely recognized by most young people. *Tipico* is a traditional form of Panamanian music. Bands consist of a guitar, an accordion, and some percussion instrument(s), plus a singer. It is quite similar to American country music, with lyrics often relating to romance and life's various hardships. Jamaican reggae, Latin salsa and meringue, and Northern American jazz also are quite popular. On the Caribbean coast, African music, song, and dance are popular. With nearly 250 radio and approximately 40 television broadcast stations, a steady fare of electronic entertainment is available. Panamanians also enjoy dancing and other arts.

The country has a number of museums and art galleries that residents enjoy. Folk arts in particular—baskets, ceramics, textiles, jewelry, and visual arts—are popular and of high quality. In larger cities, theaters provide a variety of entertainment. Many Panamanians, of course, simply prefer to be entertained at home with family and friends. Simple conversation and dining are popular. Men will often gather with their friends at a neighborhood *cantina* (bar). Women may gather for casual conversation that often focuses upon home and family. They also may sew, make crafts, or cook.

HEALTH

An American military major, Dr. Walter Reed, following a theory developed several decades earlier by a Cuban physician, confirmed that dreaded yellow fever is transmitted by mosquitoes. His discovery, at the beginning of the twentieth century, made it possible to lessen the threat of this often deadly disease and thereby continue work on the Panama Canal.

Among Latin American mainland countries, Panama has a fairly good health record, ranking among the most favorable five or six states within the region. In such critical areas as physicians per capita and life expectancy, Panama ranks quite high. Its infant mortality rate and percentage of adults testing positive for HIV/AIDS are quite low.

Access to adequate health care and hygiene varies from region to region. Facilities and sanitation tend to be inadequate in many of Panama's more remote rural areas and small towns. Panama has a national public health program, and as one would expect, the best medical personnel and facilities are in the larger urban centers, such as Panama City, Colón, and David. Free examinations, sanitation programs (most of the country has clean drinking water), and health care are provided for those who are unable to afford it. Many physicians were trained in the United States and the quality of care in the major hospitals and clinics is comparable to that available in the United States. Relatively inexpensive health insurance is available and the price is low because the cost of medical care is much lower than in the United States. Also, laws prohibit frivolous lawsuits against healthcare providers, thereby keeping the cost of medical malpractice insurance low. Prescription drugs also cost much less in Panama than in North America. Many of them can be purchased over-the-counter, without a prescription, which contributes to additional savings.

EDUCATION

Panama has an official literacy rate of about 92 percent, a figure that has risen steadily and continues to do so. In the cities, it is much higher; in rural areas, somewhat lower. The folk, you will recall, are often unable to read or write. *Education* can be defined as "learning for living." What a rural *campesino* and a successful urban resident need to know in order to survive and thrive within their respective settings differ greatly. Many illiterate peasants are extremely knowledgeable in terms of surviving within their rural environment and folk culture. In fact, several decades ago, NASA hired a Panamanian Amerindian, from a remote tribe, to teach astronauts tropical survival techniques. In this "Stone Age" meets "Space Age" arrangement, the Amerindian possessed a wealth of practical knowledge that our very-well educated astronauts needed to know.

In Panama, primary education is compulsory for children between the ages of 7 and 15. It is also free. After completing their primary schooling, about 3 of every 4 youngsters continue on to enroll in secondary school programs. Again, the number is considerably higher for students living in urban areas and much lower in the countryside. Many rural families simply are too poor to send their youngsters on to secondary school. They are unable to pay the cost of transportation, school supplies and uniforms, and possibly room and board while living away from home (most secondary schools are in larger communities). Secondary schools offer students several options. Some students follow a vocational training program. Among the options are courses that prepare them for careers in such fields as agriculture, commerce, various industrial trades, or the arts. Others prefer a general curriculum that prepares graduates for admission to a college or university.

After graduating from secondary school, a small number of Panamanians continue their education. If they can afford it, some go to colleges in the United States or elsewhere. Most, however, opt for specialized training in one of several vocational schools, or enter one of Panama's several universities. The largest institution of higher learning is University of Panama, located in Panama City. It has a huge campus and a student enrollment of nearly 75,000. The country's major private institution is the Catholic University of Santa Maria la Antigua, also in Panama City. There are several other church-supported colleges in Panama.

SPORTS

Team sports are popular throughout Panama. As is true throughout Latin America (and much of the rest of the world), the most popular team sport is *futból*. (Only in the United States and Canada is "football" played the North American way; elsewhere, "football" is what we call soccer.) Throughout the country, youngsters can be seen playing the game at every opportunity and on nearly any open spot. During recent decades, Panamanians have successfully adopted several sports associated with the United States, including basketball and baseball. Panama has produced some excellent players including Baseball Hall of Famer Rod Carew and New York Yankees relief pitcher Mariano Rivera. The country also has produced some excellent boxers, including Roberto Durán, who was a champion in four weight classes. Fishing, tennis, cycling, horse racing, and cockfighting are also popular.

By nearly any measure, Panamanians are better off today than at any previous time. Government is relatively stable, the economy is growing at a brisk pace, and with construction underway for enlarging the Panama Canal, prosperity will continue. In the next and final chapter, we will examine what the future may hold for Panama and its more than 3 million citizens.

CHAPTER

7

Panama Looks Ahead

Throughout most of its history, Panama has been a troubled land. Most of its people suffered and foreign lands—particularly Spain, and later Colombia and the United States—controlled the country's political destiny. Even as an independent country, it was poorly governed much of the time. Its people were mainly poor and powerless. A small handful of individuals controlled the keys to both power and wealth. Disease was rampant and often fatal. Much of the country was unsettled or sparsely settled by people who practiced a very traditional, self-sufficient, folk culture. Only at the isthmus, the narrow, 30-mile (50-kilometer) wide sliver of land separating the Atlantic and Pacific oceans, have some Panamanians prospered.

We will attempt to gaze into a "crystal ball" in an attempt to foresee Panama's future. Unlike many of its neighbors, Panamanians do not need to worry about most natural hazards. Devastating earthquakes, volcanic eruptions, and hurricanes rarely if ever strike the isthmus. Many of the deadly diseases can be prevented, or their vectors eradicated. Panama is home to some of the world's best tropical medicine specialists. With a clustered population (in the area of the canal), it is much easier to spray for insects, for example, than in an area with widely dispersed settlement.

Panama does face several major environmental problems. The country's forests are disappearing at an alarming rate, as is much of its wildlife. Recognizing the importance of its flora and fauna, the country has been a leader in placing lands in parks and preserves. Soils also are suffering from erosion and a loss of fertility. Although of environmental concern, the importance of agriculture (hence soil quality) to Panama's economy is dropping sharply. A possibly warming planet will not directly affect the country in serious ways. A sharp accompanying drop in precipitation, however, could be extremely damaging. It could hinder both the Panama Canal, which relies on water to operate the locks, and economic development and population growth in Panama City and environs. Pollution, too, is a growing problem. Fortunately, with a booming economy, Panama will have the capital resources to successfully address most, if not all, of its environmental issues.

It is impossible, of course, to foresee history. The senior author, however, believes that "A people who live a good geography will leave a good history." What is known is that throughout most of its history, Panama has been a troubled land. The country and its citizens have been beset with turbulent politics, economics, and social conditions. Today, however, the country is self-governed, relatively stable politically, booming economically, and relatively cohesive socially. Assuming these conditions continue, Panama's future history should be much better than that documenting its past.

Geographers often look to the past in an attempt to forecast the future. This method can help us project future trends

With improved access to public education, Panama's literacy rate has risen to 92 percent, though the statistics differ in more rural areas, where children must hike over hills and through rivers to arrive at the local school. In 2005, the United Nations International Children's Emergency Fund (UNICEF) helped set up community schools to increase educational opportunities for Panama's rural children.

in Panama's population, settlement, and culture. The rate of natural population increase has dropped sharply during recent decades, as has the fertility rate. This drop almost certainly will continue. Among the chief influences will be a continued trend of rural-to-urban migration. City dwellers, statistically, have many fewer children than do rural families. Also, urban dwellers are better educated, women are better integrated into the economy, and people tend to be less family oriented (in terms of numbers of children).

Panama City is a regional success story in many ways. The city, today, has an estimated population of more than 1.2 million. Few cities in Latin America can match Panama City's ongoing economic development and related population growth. Certainly the canal in general and Panama City in particular will continue to draw tens of thousands of people. With work underway on the canal's expansion, it is doubtful that native Panamanians can fill the thousands of new jobs. If true, Panama can expect to experience a sharp increase in immigrants from throughout Latin America and, perhaps, beyond.

Culturally, our crystal ball shows an increase in the percentage of English-speaking Panamanians. Increasingly, Panama becomes evermore involved in the global economy. Call centers, tourists and those catering to them, international business persons, scientists, and many others today rely on English. It has become the global *lingua franca*, or common tongue, in which they can communicate with one another. Roman Catholicism will remain the dominant religion, but it will continue to lose its political and social influence as the population continues to urbanize. (Rural people tend to be much more devout in their faith than are urban residents.) Protestantism, and perhaps other faiths, will continue to chip away at the percentage of the population that is Catholic. Sharpest gains will be made by fundamentalist, charismatic faiths, a trend occurring throughout much of the less-developed countries (LDCs). As Panama continues to undergo the transition from an LDC to a developed country, it will further expand its global ties. During coming decades, the country will become even more cosmopolitan in its culture and outlook.

The key to any country's prosperity and the well-being of its citizens rests in the combined success (or failure) of its political and economic systems. Historically, Panama, like many other LDCs, was handicapped by bad government. Since 1989, the country has enjoyed a democratic government and relative political stability. Corruption is still widespread, as it is in many LDCs, but there are signs that conditions are improving. Political stability may be the single most important factor contributing to economic growth. This certainly appears to be true in the case of Panama. The country has enjoyed unparalleled economic development and prosperity since democracy was restored.

When thinking about Panama and its economy, it is easy to consider only the canal and its importance. This is a mistake. During recent years, Panama has taken strong steps to diversify its economy. Today, the service sector is booming. Tourism is experiencing rapid growth, including a 68-story hotel and resort planned by American developer, Donald Trump. Rival developers have plans in the works to build the tallest structure in all of Latin America in Panama City. American retirees are now flocking to Panama as a place of residence. Occidental Petroleum Corporation has proposed a $7 billion oil refining project in Panama. If built, the facility would process 350,000 barrels of crude oil a day. And a new container port is opening near the Pacific entrance to the canal. These are just some of the economic developments underway or to come.

In late 2007, Panama's economy was estimated to be growing by 8 to 11 percent annually (depending upon the source of information). According to LatinSource, a leading economic consulting group, Panama is experiencing the fastest economic growth in all of Latin America. This growth is projected to continue in the foreseeable future. Certainly construction activities related to the canal's expansion will boost the economy. So, too, will the canal's greatly expanded capacity once work is completed. Meanwhile, Panama's economy continues to diversify and develop with no slowing in sight.

By any measure, it appears that life in Panama is going to improve, and improve greatly, during the coming decades.

As a country in development, Panama is trying to improve its economy and country by increasing access to information and education that could lead to jobs and opportunities for Panamanians. Information centers like this one is one example of some of the national campaigns the government has enacted to help improve the lives of its citizens.

In the previous chapter it was mentioned that the country currently ranks fifty-eight among the 177 countries rated in the Human Development Index listing. Certainly this position will improve in the years to come. Again, the key to progress is a stable government and a growing economy. Today, Panama appears to have both ingredients to success working in its favor. With additional revenue, education, health care, infrastructure, and other services can be improved. Conditions in the rural villages and countryside can be improved. When things are going well, they do so to nearly everyone's benefit.

Looking ahead, the authors are willing to go out on a limb. We believe that Panama has an extremely bright future. Assuming present trends continue, the country's prospects may be as good, if not better, than that of nearly any other Latin American country. After centuries of hardship, many, if not most, Panamanians can look to their country's future, as well as to that of their own and their children, with considerable optimism, confidence, and pride.

Facts at a Glance

Physical Geography

Location Central America, bordering both the Caribbean Sea and the North Pacific Ocean, between Colombia and Costa Rica

Area Total: 30,193 square miles (78,200 square kilometers); slightly smaller than South Carolina; land: 47,217 square miles (75,990 square kilometers); water: 1,373 square milies (2,210 square kilometers)

Boundaries Total: 344.8 miles (555 kilometers); border countries: Colombia, 139.8 miles (225 kilometers), Costa Rica, 205 miles (330 kilometers)

Coastlines 1,547 miles (2,490 kilometers)

Climate Wet tropical with small area of wet-and-dry tropical on Pacific side; hot, humid, cloudy; prolonged rainy season (May to January), short dry season (January to May)

Terrain Isthmus; interior mostly steep, rugged mountains and dissected, upland plains; coastal areas largely plains and rolling hills

Elevation Extremes Lowest point is the Pacific Ocean at sea level; highest point is the Volcán Barú at 11,398 feet (3,474 meters) above sea level

Land Use Arable land, 7.26%; permanent crops, 1.95%; forest & other, 90.79% (2005)

Irrigated Land 267 square miles (430 square kilometers) (2003)

Natural Hazards Few; occasional severe showers with accompanying wind; forest fires in the Darién area

Natural Resources Copper, mahogany forests, shrimp, hydropower

Environmental Issues Water pollution from agricultural runoff threatens fishery resources; deforestation of tropical rain forest; land degradation and soil erosion threatens siltation of Panama Canal; air pollution in urban areas; mining threatens environmental destruction

People

Population 3,242,173; males, 1,637,699; females, 1,604,474 (July 2007 est.)

Population Growth Rate 1.564% (2007 est.)

Net Migration Rate -0.37 migrant(s)/1,000 population (2007 est.)

Fertility Rate	2.66 children born/woman (2007 est.)
Birthrate	21.45 births/1,000 population (2007 est.)
Death Rate	5.44 deaths/1,000 population (2007 est.)
Life Expectancy at Birth	Total population: 75.2 years; male, 72.7 years; female, 77.8 years (2007 est.)
Median Age	Total: 26.4 years; male, 26 years; female, 26.7 years (2007 est.)
Ethnic Groups	Mestizo (mixed Amerindian and white), 70%; Amerindian and mixed (West Indian), 14%; white, 10%; Amerindian, 6%
Religion	Roman Catholic, 85%; Protestant, 15%
Language	Spanish (official); English 14%; Note: Many Panamanians are bilingual
Literacy	(Age 15 and over can read and write) Total population: 91.9% (male, 92.5%; female, 91.2%) (2000 census)

Economy

Currency	Balboa; U.S. Dollar
GDP Purchasing Power Parity (PPP)	$29.14 billion (2007 est.)
GDP Per Capita	$9,000 (2007 est.)
Labor Force	1.471 million Note: shortage of skilled labor, but an oversupply of unskilled labor (2007 est.)
Unemployment Rate	7.2% (2007 est.)
LaborForce by Occupation	Services, 67% (2006 est.); industry, 18%; agriculture, 15%
Agricultural Products	Bananas, rice, corn, coffee, sugarcane, vegetables; livestock; shrimp
Industries	Construction, brewing, cement and other construction materials, sugar milling
Exports	$9.662 billion f.o.b.; Note: includes the Colon Free Zone (2007 est.)
Imports	$12.1 billion f.o.b. (includes the Colon Free Zone) (2007 est.)
Leading Trade Partners	Exports: U.S., 39.8%; Spain, 8.1%; Netherlands, 6.7%; Sweden, 5.6%; Costa Rica, 4.5%; (2006) Imports: U.S., 27%; Netherlands Antilles, 10.1%; Costa Rica, 5.1%; Japan, 4.7% (2006)

Export Commodities	Bananas, shrimp, sugar, coffee, clothing
Import Commodities	Capital goods, foodstuffs, consumer goods, clothing
Transportation	Roadways: 7,234 miles (11,643 kilometers), 2,502 miles (4,208 kilometers) is paved (2000); Railways: 220.5 miles (355 kilometers); Airports: 116; 54 are paved runways
Ports and Terminals	Balboa, Colón, Cristobal

Government

Country name	Conventional long form: Republic of Panama; conventional short form: Panama
Capital City	Panama City
Type of Government	Constitutional democracy
Head of Government	President Martin Torrijos Espino
Independence	Became independent from Spain, November 28, 1821; gained independence from Colombia, November 3, 1903
Administrative Divisions	9 provinces (provincias, singular—provincia) and 1 territory (comarca); Bocas del Toro, Chiriqui, Cocle, Colón, Darién, Herrera, Los Santos, Panama, San Blas (Kuna Yala), and Veraguas

Communications

TV Stations	38 (1998)
Radio Stations	235 (AM, 101; FM, 134)
Telephones	2,126,900 (including 1,694,000 cell phones)
Internet Users	220,000 (2006)

*Source: *CIA-The World Factbook* (2007)

B.C.

<20,000 (?) Earliest humans may have reached and passed through Panama by either land or coastal route.

11,000 (?) Archaeological evidence of earliest humans in Panama.

A.D.

1502 Spanish explorer Rodrigo de Bastidas first known European to reach Panama.

1510 Martin Fernández de Encisco founded Santa Maria de la Antigua del Darién, the first successful European settlement on the American mainland.

1513 Vasco Nuñez de Balboa crosses the isthmus to "discover" the Pacific Ocean (from the eastern edge of the basin).

1519 Panama becomes Spanish Vice-royalty of New Andalucia.

1821 Panama gains independence from Spain and joins the confederacy of Gran Colombia that includes Bolivia, Colombia, Ecuador, Peru, and Venezuela.

1830 Gran Colombia dissolves, and Panama becomes part of Colombia.

1846 Panama and the United States reach an agreement allowing the United States to construct a railway crossing the Isthmus of Panama.

1855 Transisthmian railroad completed (it was the first to span a continent).

1878 In 1880, the French, under Ferdinand de Lesseps, began construction of a sea-level canal across the Isthmus of Panama.

1889 French attempt to build canal was abandoned because of financial problems and the deaths of some 22,500 workers.

1903 Panama gains independence from Colombia and becomes a U.S. protectorate; the United States gains permission to build the Panama Canal and is granted permanent control of the Canal Zone.

1914 Forty-eight mile (77-kilometer) long Panama Canal is completed and opened to shipping, reducing by about

8,000 miles (12,875 km) the Atlantic-Pacific distance around the southern tip of South America. An estimated 5,000 workers died during the U.S. construction of the canal, most of whom perished from malaria and yellow fever (an estimated 27,000 to 28,000 died during the combined French and U.S. construction projects).

1939 Panama ceases to be a United States protectorate.

1968 General Omar Torrijos Herrera overthrows the elected president and establishes a dictatorship that lasts until 1981.

1977 The United States agrees to transfer the canal to Panama on December 31, 1999.

1982 Most oil tankers too large to pass through Panama Canal; a pipeline is built across the isthmus to transport Alaskan crude oil from Pacific to Atlantic ports.

1983 General Manuel Noriega becomes commander of Panama's military and, although never being elected to the office of president, he controls the country as a military dictator until 1989.

1989 U.S. forces invade Panama and arrest Noriega on federal charges of cocaine trafficking, money laundering, and racketeering. He was convicted in 1992 and imprisoned in the United States.

1991 Panama's parliament approves constitutional reforms.

1999 Panama elects Mireya Moscoso Rodríguez as its first woman president (she served until 2004).

1999 On December 31, Panama gains complete control of the Panama Canal.

2006 Panamanian voters approve a referendum to spend $5.2 billion to upgrade the Panama Canal.

2006 Panama and the United States agree upon a free trade arrangement between the two countries.

2007 Work begins on enlarging the Panama Canal, which will double its current capacity; scheduled for completion by 2014–2015.

Collier, Simon, Thomas E. Skidmore, and Harold Blakemore, eds. *The Cambridge Encyclopedia of Latin America and the Caribbean.* Cambridge: Cambridge University Press, 1992.

CultureGrams. *Republic of Panama.* Ann Arbor, Mich.: ProQuest, 2007 (annual editions).

Embassy of the Republic of Panama, 2862 McGill Terrace, NW, Washington, D.C. 2008 (various data).

James, Preston E., and C. W. Minkel. *Latin America.* Hoboken, N.J.: John Wiley & Sons, 1986.

Sauer, Carl O. *The Early Spanish Main.* Berkeley and Los Angeles: University of California Press, 1967.

West, Robert C., and John P. Augelli. *Middle America: Its Lands and Peoples.* Englewood Cliffs, N.J.: Prentice Hall, 1989.

Further Reading

Baker, Christopher, and Gilles Mingasson. *National Geographic Traveler: Panama*. Washington, D.C.: National Geographic Society, 2007.

Firestone, Matthew. *Panama*. Oakland, Calif.: Lonely Planet, 2007.

Gritzner, Charles F. *Latin America*. New York: Chelsea House, 2006.

Schreck, Kristina. *Frommer's Panama*. Hoboken, N.J.: John Wiley & Sons, 2007.

Snyder, Sandra T. *Living in Panama*. Panama City: TanToes, S.A., Panama Relocation Services, 2007.

Web sites

About.com
http://geography.about.com/

BBC News (timeline)
http://news.bbc.co.uk/2/hi/americas/country_profiles/1229333.stm

CIA—The World Factbook (Panama)
http://www.cia.gov/cia/publications/factbook/

Countries and Their Cultures-Panama
http://www.everyculture.com/No-Sa/Panama.html

Country Reports
http://www.countryreports.org/

Ethnologue—Languages of Panama
http://www.ethnologue.com/show_country.asp?name=Panama

Infoplease: Panama
http://www.infoplease.com/ipa/A0107870.html

Lonely Planet
http://www.lonelyplanet.com/worldguide/destinations/central-america/panama

Nations Online: Panama
http://www.nationsonline.org/oneworld/panama.htm

Panama Canal Authority
http://www.pancanal.com/eng/

United Nations Development Programme—Human Development Index (Report)
http://hdr.undp.org/en/statistics/

U.S. Department of State, Background Notes: Panama
http://www.state.gov/r/pa/ei/bgn/2030.htm

U.S. Library of Congress, Country Studies (Panama)
http://lcweb2.loc.gov/frd/cs/patoc.html

Wikipedia (Panama, Panama Canal, or other specific topic)
www.wikipedia.org
http://en.wikipedia.org/wiki/Panama_Canal

Picture Credits

Index

Index

About the Contributors

CHARLES F. GRITZNER is distinguished professor of geography at South Dakota State University in Brookings. He is now in his fifth decade of college teaching and research. In addition to classroom instruction, he enjoys traveling, writing, working with teachers, and sharing his love of geography with readers. As a senior consulting editor for Chelsea House Publishers' *Modern World Nations* and *Major World Cultures* series, he has a wonderful opportunity to combine each of these "hobbies." Dr. Gritzner has served as both president and executive director of the National Council for Geographic Education and has received the Council's highest honor, the George J. Miller award for Distinguished Service to Geographic Education, as well as other honors from the NCGE, Association of American Geographers, and other organizations.

LINNEA C. SWANSON is a geography major at South Dakota State University. She plans to pursue a Ph.D. and an academic career in the field. Linnea was raised on a farm near the small town of Lake Norden, South Dakota. Growing up in the country with three older brothers nurtured her enjoyment of exploring and the outdoors. Traveling is one of her favorite activities. She particularly enjoys meeting local people along the way, listening to their stories, and learning about their ways of life. She enjoys experiencing various kinds of music and food from the different regions of the United States and around the world. As a young geographer, Linnea looks forward to exploring our fascinating world and learning more about its varied people and places for decades to come.

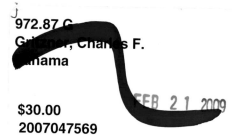

DATE DUE

SONG Smith 2011	
BETH 6.3-2013	WITHDRAWN
JUN 0 5 2013	
APLW 2.8.2018	
WITHDRAWN	
WITHDRAWN	